Business of Technology
and
Wisdom of Nature

Prafull Verma
Kavindra Sharma

Business of Technology and Wisdom of Nature
Copyright © 2020 by Prafull Verma and Kavindra Sharma

All rights reserved. No part of this book may be reproduced or transmitted in any form or by any means without written permission from the author.

ISBN (9798648502017)

Dedication

To the victims of abused technology and to the people who believe that the world needs wisdom more than the world needs technology, and to those whose admiration and respect for Nature exceeds their excitement with technology.

Table of Content

PREFACE 1
INTRODUCTION 5
THINKING AND REASONING 9
RISE OF UNREASON 29
TECHNOLOGY INVENTIONS 45
LIMITATIONS OF TECHNOLOGY 67
DOES TECHNOLOGY MAKE PEOPLE DUMB? 79
WHERE TECHNOLOGY IS TAKING US? 85
TECHNOLOGY IS ARTIFICIAL BY DESIGN 95
TECHNOLOGY IS LARGELY SELF SERVING 115
WHAT TECHNOLOGY PROMOTES? 125
WISDOM 139
WISDOM AND KNOWLEDGE 147
WISDOM OF NATURE 153
WISDOM OF CROWD 163
WISDOM IN BUSINESS 169
REAL VALUE OF TECHNOLOGY 175
LESSONS FROM HISTORY 183
EPILOGUE 185

Preface

Technology is a vast field and each Industry has its own set of technologies. But the most common and sometimes most important piece of technology of a modern enterprise is Information Technology (IT). In industries like Banking and Insurance, IT is a major driver of business as well. Across industries, many common business functions like, Accounting and Finance, HR, Administration, Customer relationship management, etc., are driven by information technology. The financial industry also runs completely on information technology.

A business is fundamentally a collection of business processes, which are excellently represented by IT in order to execute them more effectively and efficiently on computers. In the past few decades, we have actually witnessed how information technology in enterprise is developed, deployed and run, from business enabler function to the core business function. Gone are the old days when the CEO would leave technology matters to the CIO. Likewise, boards of directors are compelled to bring in technology-savvy CEOs. But how many CEOs or CIOs are technology-savvy in the real sense? Whether a blind man is leading another blind man? Are there vested interests that promote technology beyond its actual utility? We pondered over such questions and with our experiences, we have formed opinions that are a blend of philosophy with technology. We have discussed, argued, thought-through and analyzed many real-life and anecdotal situations relating to technology, Nature and wisdom.

In this book we are focusing on IT as the technology with a blend of philosophy. In addition to the experiences in enterprise IT and business environments, our point of view (PoV) is also from the experience of living in diversified places, societies and cultures. Notwithstanding the fact that we are writing in the context of information technology, our core ideas and theories also apply to other technologies.

We also believe that change is natural and thus the progress in society is also natural but for every change, Nature has defined a pace of change. Our primary focus is to challenge the artificial acceleration of the change fueled by technology. In other words, our observation that the movement away from Nature has become the primary purpose of technology is a concern.

Life today is unthinkable without technology. But increasing focus on commercial aspects leading to exploitation of consumers (people), and gradual decline of people's own thinking capabilities and their short-sightedness, are the main triggers to write this book. People's appetite for consumption is increasing dramatically. In addition to the desire to consume more, there is a rise in the culture of instant gratification. Consumers want more, and they want it now. Traditional use of technology cannot fulfill this appetite and humans have moved towards unwise and unnatural (ab)use of technology. We have drawn a lot of inspiration from Nature, and established that wisdom is the most fundamental aspect of being human and hence it is beyond the realms of technology.

Businesses today are synonymous with technology and cannot exist and cannot thrive without it. We get most of our technology through businesses. Business, and thus technology is mainly for its own profit and growth, so we called it Business of Technology in the title. Our wisdom, which comes as being thinking human beings, is intimately connected with Nature as we are *supposed to* be part of Nature. So, Wisdom of Nature is another part of the title -- and all these four aspects, that is Business, Technology, Nature and Wisdom have many intricate connections that this book explores.

This book is likely to expose some inconvenient truths---and we are the part of that system that probably does not want to hear the truth but live with illusion due to obsession with technology. We also admire technology, provided that it is used wisely. The authors have spent long years in the IT Industry and owe it most of their knowledge, wisdom and friends. Being critical and at times harsh on our own industry is all with good intentions to raise the level of thinking instead of just accepting the status quo and going with the flow.

Every language has some unique words and phrases that have no exact equivalent in other languages. We have used certain words and phrases of Hindi Language due the precision with which they express certain ideas and notions. But there are only a few of them and we have given English language equivalent words in the context to ensure high fidelity in the translation and there is no material impact on the understanding of readers who do not know the Hindi terminology. For example, the translation of "*Dharma*" is "righteousness" in English but certainly it is not the precise and accurate communication of the meaning expressed by *Dharma*.

Acknowledgement

We owe this book primarily to interactions with our colleagues, competitors, collaborators in our respective IT organizations that we have been part of, and to the academic fraternity of students, research scholars, professors, etc., who have questioned and enriched many of our thoughts and point-of-views. Special thanks to Col. Ranjit Chitale who painstakingly proof-read and suggested syntactic and semantics corrections.

Individually we would like to thank our wives Annie and Chetna for their immense support on home front during this lock-down period. Our kids Naomi, Prateek, Pritha have heard us talking about many of the stories and episodes on the dinner table and their mere act of listening and questioning has made us think and re-think several aspects mentioned in the book.

Introduction

This is the age of buzzwords and jargon---and incidentally most jargon is related to information technology. Buzzwords are manufactured, traded, and promoted, to develop a shallow layer of appealing presentation and hide poor performance on the past promises. Every time a technology fails to deliver the overcommitted performance, more buzzwords are manufactured to make new promises and renew the reason to be in business. Since IT is at the core of every business, the buzzwords of IT have become a common factor across all industries. A few years ago, a CEO of the top company in the financial industry even made a famous statement "we are a technology company who happen to be in the business of finance". Most of the energy and efforts are put into the buzzword business and little is left to do the real work. We hear words like AI (Artificial Intelligence), ML (Machine Learning), Deep-learning, Blockchain, Digital, etc. A few years back the buzzwords were Cloud, Data-warehousing, Pay-per-use, etc., and further back they were Client-server Architecture, Outsourcing, Offshoring, Linux, Object Oriented Programming, Java, MVC (Model-View-Controller), Design Patterns, etc.

So, buzzwords have always been around, and the IT industry is famous or notorious for them. In the past, IT buzzwords were used by IT professionals or people intimately connected with IT.

Nowadays, these buzzwords are used by everyone across industries - managers, CEOs or Board members, stock-market analysts, journalists - nearly by all 'Market Makers'. Annual reports of all companies will mention Digital, Deep-learning etc. CEOs will make it a point, particularly in media interviews to emphasize how Blockchains will revolutionize their industry and every other industry. Probably only the lowest level worker in the IT industry has not taken fancy to these buzzwords, because real IT is quite different and few among them get to work on these technologies. Basically, it establishes the fact that IT is central to all businesses, so competitiveness of a business depends largely on its IT, which makes CEOs, company boards and market analysts talk about it. How much they really know and how sure they are to embrace these technologies in their real business is questionable. Everyone is happy with shallow knowledge and bold statements when engaging in conversations using these buzzwords---except for the true experts who know the reality but are often tongue-tied and shy.

We will get to some fundamental aspects of the whole thinking and reasoning process and how some flaws are creeping into it. This book deals with how inaptly we are dealing with technology and use of technology (Information Technology to be precise) – within corporations and within our personal lives. Our point-of-view has emerged from experience, and we do not expect all our perspectives to be taken at face value by the reader. Our humble attempt is to make one think – think deeply and sincerely before simply embracing a technology without introspecting. There are trade-offs in life for everything, and technology is no exception. But have we traded too much to get too little? Have we become very shallow in our understanding of technology and its fundamentals? Do we simply think technology is only a utility and nothing beyond? Questions like these may pop-up in your mind when you read this book – and that is the main objective. You may get some answers, you may agree to some point-of-views, or you may entirely dismiss our position – all these are acceptable modes of thinking.

And then we extend these ideas to the notion of *wisdom*, which is independent of technology. We are smarter with technology on our side, but are we wiser than before, wiser than our previous generations? And collectively, as a team, as a society or as democracy, are we really smarter or wiser than before in spite of all the technology at our fingertips? What is, and what should be the role of the media, social as well as conventional one, that uses the latest Information and communication technology?

And then we take a pause admiring Nature. All life, humans, animals, plants, etc., exist within   Nature. Barring humans, all other life forms are fully dependent on Nature. There are many beautiful and magical things that we all admire about Nature, and we also know its amazing power. Einstein once famously quoted "Look deep into Nature, and then you will understand everything better". Most great scientists fully subscribed to the beauty and power of Nature in one way or another, with or without bringing God in the equation. But perhaps due to over-reliance on technology and due to our own short-sightedness, we are fast separating away from Nature. Although we search for meaning and purpose of life – and it is very disturbing but thought provoking to note that barring us humans, Nature has plans and purpose for every creature on the Earth. Nature includes all creatures in its grand scheme of things, but humans have chosen to be out of that scheme — mainly relying on intelligence, rational thinking and technology. We are using technology as a replacement of Nature in many situations, which is questionable. While technology has its own place in our personal and corporate lives, helping us and enabling us to accomplish more with less, we have become excessively greedy (or stupid), and allowed technology to occupy the central role in our lives. We are fast losing control and leaving the crucial decision-making in the hands of technology. Technology is a great enabler, but is it going to be a great master as well? This book talks about wisdom in such context.

We have certain point-of-views on such matters, which you will find interspersed in the book. Although this book is not intended to give any direct answers to many questions, it will try to make you think by giving you hints through stories and experiences.

Thinking and Reasoning

My thought is me: that is why I cannot stop thinking. I exist because I think; I cannot keep from thinking.

Jean-Paul Sartre

We exist because we think - and we think constantly while awake. It is extremely hard to stop thinking even for some moments. Thinking is next to breathing perhaps - almost involuntary. Our thinking is driven by intentions, feelings and emotions. Thinking is an intense exercise of the mind and capability of the human brain. *"Sochana aur vicharana"* are *Hindi* language terms denoting two powerful actions: thinking and deliberating. *Sochana* is done individually and *vicharana* is done collectively with like-minded and very limited groups (2-3), and both are the act of thinking. Intensely focused deep thinking is called *Chintan-Manan*, another *Hindi* language term. It roughly translates to pondering over, reflecting and introspecting. Great scientists, litterateur, leaders, spent a great deal of time in *Chintan-Manan* - imagining possibilities and hypothesizing conjectures. Thinking is deep rooted in life itself and is a unique gift to mankind, as we would like to believe.

Vivek is another Hindi word that has some element of wisdom and it means reasoning, which is a logical approach of thought process that brings in rationality in the thinking. Thinking is a broad term, generally referring to all conscious activity of the mind. Reasoning is a particular type, mode, category, or kind of thought, specifically and intentionally focused on logical problem solving or rational thought. Do we need to think to reason? Most reasoning today is not based on any thinking. Right thinking is more important than thinking correctly.

Number-crunching, which is also part of human capability related to thinking, but it is just a small part of it. These days, we hear technology like Alexa and Watson that appear to be thinking and doing some amazing tasks. But in essence, they are only doing some sort of number-crunching based computation. Watson was shown to be able to debate on a topic with human-like abilities and gave view-points based on vast amounts of information - it could search on the Internet and make a logical set of observations pertaining to a topic. It also helps Oncologists in treating cancer patients with specific line of treatment. These are all noteworthy contributions of Computer Science leveraged by a commercially available technology - at least that's what is being claimed.

In earlier days (1960 or so), when computers started appearing as a great technological breakthrough (which they are), the possibility of whether it could prove theorems was explored. As we know, theorem proving was considered to be human ability, deducing logical conclusions in a stepwise manner using already proven facts or lemmas, etc. Similarly, playing chess was considered to be a task involving real and hard thinking. Theorem proving was done long back and chess is also mastered by the computers. But actually, these are computational tasks and computation is just one part of thinking. In fact, now we believe that computation is better done by computers so what remains for humans is real thinking which is based on feelings, fueled by imagination, and driven by intentions and emotions of human beings. A human being can think "Why am I here on this planet earth?" "What is the purpose of Life and this creation? etc. And in this search he will experiment, will seek, will learn, will challenge, will develop faith, will develop biases, and will develop science & technology as well. All these aspects of thinking are not in the realm of computers. Though we can inject some *feelings* in computers in an artificial way -- like a computer can be programmed to appear sad on seeing an accident. But it will be all without any feeling.

An aspect of thinking called *logical thinking* can be done by computers since a logic can be mathematically represented (modeled) within a computer. So, when bombarded with hundreds of facts and hundreds of rules (logic) to make a decision, computers can do such logical thinking much faster and in a consistent manner. If one can *model or transform* a problem to be a computational or logical problem, computers will be better at solving it - and that is surely a gift to the modern world. Now we do not have to tax our brains for complex number crunching, or store, recall and traverse a long list of facts and rules to arrive at some logical decision.

Science and mathematics are the core elements of all technologies, and are developed on the foundation of thinking followed by rethinking. Science has progressed on thinking and arriving at the correct conclusion, and then rethinking and proving it incorrect, and then again arriving at the new and (probably in this iteration) correct conclusion. A conversation between Albert Einstein and his student illustrates this –

"Student: Dr. Einstein, Aren't these the same questions as last year's [physics] final exam?

Dr. Einstein: Yes; But this year the answers are different."

The cycle continues to progress to the next and advanced state. Thinking not only produces the knowledge but also keeps the scope of wisdom alive and active. Without thinking, the wisdom will perish (but knowledge may not). The science and mathematics came to their modern form starting from the time of Pythagoras, Euclid and Archimedes, accelerated from the time of Galileo and Newton, and culminating perhaps to its full glory in the Einstein era. All these great scientists and mathematicians, and there were many more, were great thinkers and philosophers. It is believed that Pythagoras (570 BC) was the first man to call himself Philosopher, which meant "lover of wisdom". Philosophy is the study of general and fundamental questions about existence, knowledge, values, reason, mind, and language. Such questions are often posed as problems to be studied or resolved. The term philosophy was probably coined by Pythagoras. Science and mathematics were considered to be a part of, or branches of philosophy for the right reasons.

All early philosophers thought in the context of Nature and humanity, and gave many pearls of wisdom to common folks who could not understand their work of science or mathematics. Many of their discoveries challenged various accepted religious notions pertaining to the Earth, natural phenomenon, planetary system, etc., and some of them were even persecuted by the church and authorities. By the time the first industrial revolution arrived, science had established the firm foundation to enable it. The era of modern technology started with the second industrial revolution, which is also known as the Technological revolution and accelerated in the 20th century. And now we have the IT Revolution or Computer age whose roots are in Computer Science. There were many great Computer Scientists and thinkers like Alan Turing who gave the famous Turing test way back in 1950 to test whether or not a computer is capable of thinking like a human being. Then John Neumann gave the Stored Program concept where Data and Program (code) could both be stored in the same computer memory. Dijkstra, Donald Knuth, Alan Kay and many contributed immensely to computer science. Dennis Richie and Brian Kernighan, two programmer-scientist at Bell Labs in New Jersey, gave a unique operating system called UNIX and a unique minimalistic programming language called C using which they demonstrated that a simple "Hello World" program can be written in just 3 or 4 lines of code. This was an order of magnitude improvement over previous generation programming languages like COBOL and PL/1 where similar programs would take 50 to hundred lines of code. Unix and C were remarkably efficient and consumed very little overheads and really worked very well on the smallest to largest computers available in that era and today. That was around 1975-80 and that really led to standardization fueling the IT revolution that followed soon. All the modern versions of Operating systems, like Android, and many modern programming languages have their roots in Unix and C.

While science and mathematics have roots in philosophy and thus in Nature, technology has some roots in science and deeper connect with *business*. And business is mainly about profitability and growth. Let's consider Steve Jobs, the most admired technology leader of our time. He gave us the best of the technology in the field of general computing, mobile computing and entertainment. He was a visionary technology leader with tremendous business sense who created iTunes like amazing business model. He understood not just the customers, but the future customers who were yet to be even born, and designed his devices to the perfection in form, functionality, performance and aesthetics. Through ups-and-downs in the corporate world, he kept the interest of his company, Apple Inc., as the top most priority. Without taking away an iota of credit from him, we can say he was very sharply focused on the success of Apple Inc., which basically means its market share, profits and growth. There is nothing wrong in this. But technology, however great and useful, mainly serves narrow interests of an individual or a company, and in the process, it does create wealth, well-being and progress in the society at large. Furthermore, stakeholders benefit from it immensely, and want to promote it at any cost, with little regard to Nature and environment. The business world is all about consumers and competition where you want to win all consumers and decimate all competition. It is always a war-like situation with Mergers-&-Acquisition, antitrust law-suites, patent infringements, talent poaching, etc. Apple Inc. was no stranger and not a novice player in this arena. Again, nothing wrong here as these are perfectly accepted rules-of-the-game in a capitalist framework and business is not to be blamed here. Today, Apple products are known world-over and the company is valued at over a trillion US Dollars. But do you think it is more valuable than the simple

Pythagoras theorem discovered almost 2500 years back? Or is it more valuable than Unix and C created by two humble computer scientists in Bell Labs? Imagine if whoever made use of Pythagoras theorem in any engineering or product design, had to pay 10 cent per use - what royalty Pythagoras would earn! Probably Pythagoras would have purchased all tech giants including Apple, and would have still been left with some good change.

Each of the scientists and mathematicians mentioned here, and there were many more in each era, have produced a tremendous body of work and knowledge. They immensely contributed in the fields of scientific methods, astronomy, physics, mathematics and engineering. They wrote many books on diverse subjects, invented many devices and instruments, participated in political processes and fought with the church and authorities, contributed majorly in weaponry in warfare, and more.

Let us contrast science with technology from the perspective of their inherited "core values". Science is heavily based on thinking and experimentation, while technology is heavily based on implementation and execution. Science is like a beautiful flower in a public park whose beauty and fragrance can be admired and relished by all the passers-by. Technology is like an expensive bottle of scent, which can be bought and then used anywhere. A flower goes back to Nature, the bottle lands in a landfill.

We will talk more about core values in chapters pertaining to wisdom.

Is thinking declining in business enterprises and society?

We are staunch promoters of the approach –"First think, then plan, and then do", but finding very few takers because thinking is out of fashion in most of the business enterprises. We are observing a systematic decline of thinking culture in most of the organizations, especially in IT. Many CIOs do not think, but outsource the thinking to research analysts who in turn subcontract to product vendors. Consequently, the so-called research report becomes an instrument to advise CIO what to buy. In other words, teaching CIOs what decision to take instead of teaching how to make the right decision.

IBM immensely contributed and was pioneers of computing industry before its official birth and has many inventions and innovations to their credit. Mainframe is synonymous with IBM even today, and they gave PC to the world. But there were many more crucial and deeper innovations by IBM in all fields related to computers including its transformation into an Industry. Is it a coincidence that the decline of IBM's dominance in the market started with the decline of IBM's famous *think* culture?

IBM has built its empire on the "culture of think". Full credit goes to Thomas J. Watson Sr [1]. The THINK motto had come to Thomas J. Watson Sr. in 1911 at an early morning meeting of NCR sales managers. On this day, the managers didn't have any good ideas about how to improve the business. Frustrated, Watson strode to

---

[1] https://www.ibm.com/ibm/history/ibm100/us/en/icons/think_culture/

the front of the room and gave them a tongue-lashing. "The trouble with every one of us is that we don't think enough," he boomed. "Knowledge is the result of thought, and thought is the keynote of success in this business or any business," he told them. He decided on the spot that henceforth THINK would be the company's slogan, and ordered a subordinate to post a placard with "THINK" printed on it in bold letters on the wall of the room the following morning.

IBM THINK magazine was introduced in 1935 where Thomas J. Watson Sr. himself wrote an article "Introducing THINK". He wrote the editorial of every THINK magazine till his death in 1956. This magazine was for external publication and free distribution to all IBM customers till 1970. The approach was altered from 1971 when this magazine was made for employees only after merging with internal publication that was for employees and carried mostly the articles about the business, and the external circulation discontinued. The focus also shifted. Even though the publication continued till 1999, the relative focus and importance of THINK culture got diluted. We believe that the dominance of IBM in industry eroded because of dilution of thinking culture. Even though the IBM Think conference happens every year but that is more a matter of capitalization of the brand image rather than the spirit of THINK culture.

Application of thinking on knowledge leads to wisdom. Knowledge could be first-hand, that is based on one's own experience, or second-hand which could be acquired by books, the Internet or from other persons.

Since crowd cannot think, it cannot produce wisdom. *Therefore, the wisdom of the crowd is a faulty concept.* This can be experienced in a smaller setting like a group meeting where it is clear to most that as an individual one thinks better than the group. We will discuss this concept in details in chapter Wisdom of Crowd.

Technology is diminishing scope of thinking because the purpose of technology is to use/apply the scientific outcome established by Science, which in turn derived from thinking. Thus, the scope of thinking in the domain of technology is how to use the knowledge rather than how to produce knowledge. Since most of the time the technology is applied for commercial purposes, therefore we can say that often technology takes you away from Nature. This is fundamental to any technology since ages and justification of this core concept is sprinkled in this book in almost all chapters. Whether it is a simple thing like a timepiece, or a modern smart-phone, or super-EV, etc. At the promise of freeing you, it demands your attention and makes you addicted. It so happens that your scope and quality of thinking is directly proportional to how close you are to Nature. A simple act of walking in some natural surroundings fills you with thoughts and emotions that you cannot get while driving in a great EV or flying supersonic. Well, there is no practical option but to fly supersonic for international travel, but there also if you are on a window seat, admiring whatever natural beauty in the sky happens to be there, you are at least somewhat closer to Nature. Most people immerse themselves in their electronic devices and appear seriously busy - sometimes playing solitaire on their laptops. Jokes apart, if one cultivates the habit of finding ways to be closer to Nature., one can do so in any situation. But we are so spoiled that while walking in beautiful woods, we constantly look at our smart-phones. To substantiate all this, we will examine attributes of technology in more details in subsequent chapters about technology.

In the book *Zen and Art of Motorcycle Maintenance,* a journey on a motorcycle was very well compared with that of a car journey. On a motorcycle, you are in touch with Nature much more than within the closed confines of a car. You feel the road by the grip of your tires, can touch the road by your foot if you want, you feel natural air on your fingers and face, and all that makes you part of Nature. In the car, you are seeing the passing scenery like a TV screen in an air-conditioned cabin cut-off from Nature. It is a very subtle difference but you can feel the difference in your thought process. The thoughts are more materialistic when you are engrossed in technology, while thoughts are more holistic with a tinge of wonder when you are with Nature. I am sure all of us would have wondered looking at young kids completely immersed in their smart-phones while walking, eating, traveling or whatever. They never look up to the sky and never wonder at drifting cloud patterns or changing colors at dusk. They rarely pick-up a pebble while walking and throw it up and catch it back, as their hands and minds are already occupied with their cell-phones. All those little natural acts are gone. Technology has completely disconnected them from whatever little Nature our generation got connected to. And due to excessive exposure to information (which is a lot of junk) through smart phones, they appear to be well-informed and have an unwarranted attitude. They sure are better in handling technologies (smart-phones mainly) and adults often look up to them for some help in electronic payments or airline bookings etc., but many of them show attitude. They are not able to fathom why elders should be respected - as they appear less capable than them. This is not to blame kids but to show that technology disconnects you from Nature and this changes your thought process, quality and scope of thinking. All of us are witness and participants to a very common phenomenon in any tourist place where people are busy taking selfies and photos instead of soaking themselves in the grandeur of historical architecture or wonder of Nature. Disconnecting us from Nature seems to be the hidden agenda of technology.

Thinking and cognitive biases

In Hindi language there is a term called *Neeyat,* which roughly translates to intention but it also carries additional and important aspects of character and character-linked behavior under prevailing social conditions and norms. This is beautifully captured in a long but very meaningful childhood story, so please read on.

Once upon a time a noble king ruled his kingdom with earnest intention to make it a happy and prosperous kingdom. He cared about his subjects a lot. People were honest, happy and prosperous and living good lives. The King too was happy and was proud of the state. It was generally acknowledged that the King did not have a good council of ministers but the King directly ruled all the affairs and his competence alone was overwhelming to make his kingdom a happy and prosperous state. Time passed by, the King was getting old but he did not have any heir to succeed him. No son, no daughter. The thought of an heirless future dejected him continually and declined his interests in the affairs of the kingdom and the governance. Eventually he delegated the complete governance to some key minister and got busy in hobbies – a kind of retirement state.

Time passes by. One day the King saw a dream. In his dream he was in an open dry field in his kingdom, wolves, foxes, jackals, dogs etc. were roaming around freely. Initially he ignored, but the dream was repetitive over several days. This leads the King to believe that there is some message hidden in the dream. But he could not interpret the dream. To seek an interpretation, he announced a reward of ten thousand rupees to the person who could interpret his dream correctly. The incentive of reward brought forward many people. The King listened to their interpretation but he was not convinced so no one could win the award.

In his kingdom, there was a peasant. One hot day he was overtired and took a break resting beneath a huge banyan tree, quite away from his field. Suddenly a huge snake appeared from a root hole. He had never envisaged such a size and was stunned. Then he heard the snake telling him – "fear not; I am here to help you". Coming to his senses, the peasant asked "what kind of help?" The snake informed him about the dream of the King and the reward for its interpretation. The snake told the peasant "I will provide the correct interpretation. You convey this to the King and win the reward. But, drop five thousand rupees in this hole of mine." It was a no brainer conclusion that it makes a sound business proposition for the peasant, so he agreed.

The snake says, "here is the interpretation. Listen carefully. These animals are the symbols of pervasive conditions in the society and the message is that the characteristics of dishonesty, corruption, deception and stealing are pervasive in the kingdom. People are not hardworking but resorting to dishonest and unethical ways in life."

The peasant went to the King's palace and conveyed this interpretation. The King thought for a while and then accepted the interpretation. The peasant got the reward and the King got the message that the corruption and mismanagement from the top ministers is degrading the society.

When the peasant was returning with ten thousand rupees, he had no intention to shell out the five thousand. He weighed the consequence and concluded that there is no negative consequence. No threat from the huge snake. The snake does not know where he came from. So he decided not to go to the banyan tree at all.

The King decided to come out of retirement and took the charge again. He discovered the series of misdeeds and started undoing them. He knew that there will be chaos for a while and then things will be alright. He had good intentions and determinations. While he was bringing the things to the right track, he saw another dream. In his dream he saw a sword hanging from the roof. And of course, the King wanted the interpretation.

This time, instead of announcing the reward, he ordered the same peasant for providing the interpretation. "This time I will reward him 20 thousand rupees for the correct interpretation" the King said. So the soldiers reached his home to invite. The peasant was stunned again-this time by a real threat. He had no clue about the interpretation. A denial to the King will be considered as an act of offence and deadly consequences. While the peasant promised to come next morning, he decided to go to the snake. He visited the Banyan tree, and called for the snake. On appearance of the snake, he formally introduced himself (if the snake has forgotten!) and tendered sincere apologies. The peasant also said that the reward amount is 20 thousand rupees; so it will cover the past due of 5 thousand rupees. The snake accepted the apologies and agreed to provide the interpretation. "Listen carefully," the snake said, "there are two messages in this dream. One – there is a conspiracy cooking up to eliminate the King. Two – people are frustrated with the chaotic affairs and getting aggressive".

When the peasant delivered the message, the King thought for a while and accepted the interpretation. While the peasant got 20 thousand rupees, King got the message. It was no brainer conclusion that the displeased ministers who were once so powerful and stripped off the power are planning a coup to kill the King and take over the reign. Also, it was quite logical to conclude that people need reforms much quickly.

The peasant now with 20 thousand rupees, did not like the idea of departing 15 thousand. He again weighed the consequence. Now the snake knows him and can be dangerous. He decided to get rid of the potential danger. He bought a sword on the way and reached the banyan tree. He called the snake. When the snake appeared, he attacked it with the sword. But the snake was very careful and seemed prepared. He successfully escaped the attack and disappeared in the hole. The peasant was surprised with his failure but did not worry much about it. "Now the snake knows that I can myself be dangerous so he will not attempt any foolish act on me" he thought and went home with the full 20 thousand.

On the other side, the King took the actions on both the parts. He summoned his intelligence chief and sought investigation and proactive actions. As a result, conspirators were arrested and the potential plan was foiled before it could even take an appreciable shape. Simultaneously the King stepped up the reform efforts and expedited the welfare programs. He also monitored the progress to ensure that the result came in a timely manner.

Time passed by and the King had yet another dream. This time he saw that cows are grazing in green fields. So the peasant was called on again. "This time I will reward 40 thousand rupees for the correct interpretation" said the King. When soldiers reached the peasant's home to bring him to the palace, he had to buy the time again. This time the situation was worse. While the real and deadly consequence denial to the King was looming large, the alternate was not promising. He had already become an enemy to the snake. However, he decided to take a chance with the snake again. He went to the banyan tree, called the snake and tendered a sincere apology. He also informed the snake that the reward was 40 thousand and sure to cover every due of the past. The snake was nice indeed and pardoned him and provided the interpretation "happiness and prosperity is prevailing now. Old days are back".

The interpretation fetched the award of 40 thousand rupees to the peasant. The peasant, however, did not repeat the history. He went home, added the leftover money from the past rewards and added on top of the 40 thousand rewards and went to the banyan tree. He called the snake who appeared promptly as if he was expecting him. The peasant handed over all the money citing that he has no right to get this reward and all the rewards really belong to the snake. He also apologized once again. The snake told the peasant to keep the money as he has no use for that and also told that he does not have any complaint with him. The peasant was puzzled. He asked the snake "first time I deceived you, second time I attacked you and almost killed you, still you do not complain?"

The snake told the peasant "Remember the interpretation of the first dream? The dishonesty and corruption is prevailing in society, you just behaved likewise. The second dream was about aggressiveness and likewise you behaved, the third dream was about honesty and you behaved likewise. The fact is that your behavior was completely influenced by the prevailing conditions in the society. This is normal for an ordinary man like you. So I do not have any complaints.

While the story ends here, a significant take away is left to be discovered. If a person is not careful, he will tend to behave according to the prevailing conditions in the society unknowingly. However, we can develop capabilities to not get influenced and deliver consistent behavior according to our *Dharma* and that we will cover in chapters pertaining to wisdom.

Why are behaviors conditioned by the environmental conditions of the society? It does so, because the thinking is conditioned and that drives the behavior. Cultural aspects are a part of the social environment and they also influence thinking and it is in fact a spiral effect because thinking also feeds the culture. In artificial intelligence, we are aware of the cognitive biases and they are inevitable because the creator of the algorithms in the computers cannot be immune to cultural and environmental influences.

A picture is worth a thousand words. But sometimes words are more powerful to make you think when they are deeply connected with culture, place and time-period. Leaders deliver mostly words, so they must be very potent. Let's examine a few important words and phrases in the cultural context that always make us think.

It is worthwhile to take two examples to illustrate the sharp gap in the culture on two words namely "Divorce" and "Blasphemy".

The concept of divorce was non-existent in India till the time of invasion of foreigners in the beginning of the 12th century. Therefore, there is no exact equivalent word for divorce in any major Indian Language (Hindi and its variants, Tamil, Telugu, Malayalam, Kannada etc.). When the invaders settled in India the concept was taught and imported in the culture and today when it is an established concept, all Indian languages have either adopted the word "talaq" or created this concept with the combination of two different words (*vivah -vichchhed* in Hindi e.g. or marriage-break). Similarly, the concept of blasphemy was also non-existent because the prevailing Indian culture was highly tolerant and open.

Religious intolerance actually came to India with invaders and the concept of Blasphemy was adopted in Indian languages with the combination of two words. (*Iesh- ninda* in Hindi for example). Cognitive biases can be tackled by developing a capability that will liberate you with the influence of prevailing conditions in society and that requires a much greater level of thinking. For example, things like lobbying that are institutionalized in the USA are considered as corrupt practices in India.

Many stupidities will vanish in the world if people start thinking right. Take for example the human rights movement. We strongly believe in human rights and no sane person will disagree with the fundamental tenets behind supporting and promoting the idea. But we also believe that human rights are for humans -- not for Inhumans. The moment people think and understand the true meaning of being a "human", many stupidities that are going on under the name of human rights will just vanish.

Sometimes, inability to think promotes the wrong meaning of a word and even right meaning of a wrong word. Social distancing has become a hot theme during the lockdown of many nations because of COVID19. Actually, we do not need social distancing, we need social closeness. What we really need is physical distancing. It does not harm in this case because the perceived meaning is at least right and followed. But when the reverse happens - it is a disaster. Thus, people are practicing physical distancing in the name of social distancing. As an example, we can cite a highly miscommunicated word "secularism". The true meaning of secularism is uniform treatment regardless of the religion. However, in India, the State itself has different laws based on the religion so in true sense India is not a secular country. It was a secular country before independence! And the government who wants to make it secular is regarded as communal! Ironically people are practicing communalism in the name of secularism and vice versa.

Rise of Unreason

The whole problem with the world is that fools and fanatics are always so certain of themselves, and wiser people so full of doubts.
Bertrand Russell

We are witnessing a decline of reason and the insurgence of unreason in our society in general and its proliferation into the business world. It has enormous implications on resolution of any problem. This trend has not emerged abruptly but developed slowly over a period of time. One of the primary catalysts for the rise of unreason is people's appetite for junk opinion (just like junk food). Unfortunately, technology has fueled it by making it easy to quickly propagate bad information to a very large audience and very easy for users to consume. You can propagate an opinion from anywhere to anyone at any time; thanks to mobility and a connected world (Facebook, Twitter, WhatsApp etc.).

In the past, especially during the pre-web era, opinions were formed with depth and thoroughness of the facts and largely established through books and periodicals including newspapers' opinion columns. Corresponding to that we had IT magazines that would establish an opinion based on details. There was enough time for the opinion to get matured during the forming time itself and correction and maturity was embedded in the process of forming and propagating the opinion. With the proliferation of the web, books and white papers were diluted by blogs and in the past few years it is further diluted by tweets. Depth is a rare thing of the past.

We are now firmly in an era of immature opinions where substance is not the logic, reason and thinking behind the opinion, but the weightage that is acquired by rallying around the opinion tweets. Twitter has oversimplified the trending of opinions where depth is hidden or even non-existent. Substance is the numbers game.

You are fed with the news items or tweets that match with your preferences and biases based on past searches or web-sites that you browsed, so you see only what you would have *liked* to see. This is great and it saves your time, but it also deprives you of counter-views and other related peripheral information that is so important for all-round, holistic view-point to develop. This is evident with the increasingly polarized world as everyone gets fed with what one is looking for and what one is biased towards. AI and Machine Learning engines lurking in the background do all the work specific to a consumer (you) in feeding "convenient" information at the "convenient" time. Could be good for many things to simplify life, like telling your flight is going to be late without you enquiring, or pushing you some products that a frequent flier would need, but telling you only views favoring one political/religious party could make you very myopic and thus heavily polarized.

This trend is reflected in IT as well in the form of immature software products where the substance or value is not in the product as such, but in the weightage it acquires by getting customers rallying around it. Making a good product is not as important as developing a strong logic/algorithm, but rather a matter of building a customer base, regardless of the quality or value. It can be argued that a customer can be rallied on the basis of merit of the product but that is not necessary. It can be done by alternate skills of marketing or even buying the customer base with vested interests.

This phenomenon resonates with the phenomenon of artificial stupidity as discussed in the book – "Process Excellence for IT Operations", which was the first book authored by one of the authors of this book. The current trend is: instead of educating people on how to create an informed opinion, we teach people what opinion to make.

These are a few intriguing questions associated with the characteristics of the software industry.

1. Is there any other industry where a company can produce and sell a defective product and then charge the customer for the repair and, on top of that, may even sue its own customer?
2. Is there any other industry where customers continue to purchase overpriced product features that are unnecessary and add unwanted complexity? Is there any other industry where a customer accepts defects as the standard feature and does not demand quality? And in which producers get away with bad quality?

3. Is there any other industry that fixes the things that are not broken and, in the attempt to do so, break the things that have been working fine?

Let's take a couple of other examples from not so distant past. Everyone remembers the dot-com boom and bust around 1998-2003. Hundreds of new business models based on the Internet started emerging around the year 1995, the most prominent and generic one being the e-Commerce. IT Industry led by silicon-valley thinkers, fed to the world that the more the loss you make, the more futuristic your company is. Or, the more cash you burn, the more will be your valuation. All one should care about is the number of *Eyeballs* in such virtual businesses, which replaced *Footfalls* in Brick-and-mortar businesses. That was called *New Economy* and those who did not understand this jargon were laughed at by those who *claimed* to have understood. Valuations of companies following such doctrine went through the roof overnight while valuations of solid brick-and-mortar old-fashioned companies went down in pits. For many normal business folks this all appeared counter intuitive and *fishy*, but they also toed the line as the whole world was going that way. Soon enough, all this went bust with the market crash and normalcy was restored in the market after quite a bloodbath.

Just prior to this mega catastrophic event led by IT, there was another important event called Y2K or Year 2000, where it was believed that the world will crash on 1st Jan 2000 due to interpretation of "2000" as "00" by thousands of computer programs that were written over the last 20-30 years. These programs were written with a logic for *date, duration* and *age* calculation etc., that will assume 00 to be the year 1900. This all happened due to programmers coding the year field in two digits instead of four to save one or two bytes of memory space. And no programmer who wrote programs in, say 1985, believed or envisioned that his programs would be still used in the next century. But many programs did make it close enough to the next century with a fear that they all would crash or malfunction. Programs that dealt with insurance premium, claims settlements, interest payments, pensions, salaries, travel bookings, etc., etc., were all severely affected. An often-talked doomsday scenario was that air-traffic control programs would malfunction with the clock hitting 2000 at midnight of 1st Jan and many flying planes would drop from the sky. Anyway, we all know nothing of that sort happened since most programs were fixed in a couple of years before the year 2000. Indian IT industry and offshoring in particular, got a major boost in their business due to all this and they invented a factory model for software maintenance during this. A famous research and analyst company, had predicted many dooms-day scenarios with estimated damages of over 600 Billion US Dollars. They and many others like them made lots of money in advising clients on how to avoid Y2K bugs, whom to outsource this work to fix code, etc. When the new year day passed almost uneventfully, everyone wondered what happened to the dooms-day prediction of that research company. But public memory is short, soon everything was forgotten and they have been back in business as usual. The dot-com boom-to-bust case was a classic case of greed and herd-mentality. In case of Y2K, fear and uncertainty that was nicely packaged and sold.

Software, which is basically a computer program, is an entity, which is unlike any other entity mankind had known prior to the computer age. It has no physical properties like mass, shape, density, boiling/melting point, etc. It does not fall within laws of gravity. Software does not get fatigued or overheated like a machine part so there is no malfunction that can result from any amount of use of well-written code. And so, it was a delight for software engineers to create it easily and then keep on modifying it without any physical constraints. This freedom was greatly responsible for the rapid creation of the entire software industry as thousands of coders (programmers) could churn out billions of lines of code representing innumerable software products or functions. A software-based function can be modified by a mere coder and the modified code can be incorporated back into the system without any physical or natural constraint. Compare and contrast that with modifying and replacing a machine part inside a complex machine. You would have so many physical constraints like degree of freedom, accessibility, maneuverability, exact fitment, etc., and you would take so much trouble in making the part from cutting, machining or molding metal, etc. So, this degree of freedom that software provides is a double edge sword. Since it is very easy to create and then modify a piece of code, one could easily tamper with a piece of code with good intention but poor practices or inferior intelligence, leading to creation of faulty code and malfunctioning system. And even though we have good practices for software creation, modifications and updates etc., they are often breached or circumvented due to time-constraints or commercial considerations. In the book *The Mythical Man-month* published in 1975, many fundamental principles of software development were given with amazing clarity resulting from the experience of leading a team that created the largest software in the form of IBM's most famous Operating System OS/360 of that time. Unfortunately there are few in the Software industry who have read, and even fewer who follow the fundamental principles given in this book.

Enforcing quality in the software development process has been the toughest challenge in spite of many great tools and methodologies. It is an accepted industry belief that software will have some defects or bugs no matter how well it has been developed and tested. Is this really true? Or it is a ploy to institutionalize sub-standard products? Sometimes clients for whom the software is being developed, can make a huge difference by enforcing their own quality standards. One Japanese client did this very well by enforcing just one specific condition. The condition was with every defect found by them after we release the software, we the developers would have to find and fix five more defects! So, before we released any new version, we made doubly and triply sure by reexamining the code, thoroughness of test-cases and boundary conditions, subjected it to yet another peer review, etc. The very thought that if one defect is found by them, we will have to dig deep – very deep to unearth five more defects that may not even exist. And what if we found only three defects after a month of hard-work? That single condition changed the whole complexion of the project, the project team and even the culture at that development center. With some initial debacles, we eventually produced defect free software release after release and broke the myth of impossible. Obviously, we never signed-up for similar *cruel* and economically unviable condition with any other client but often cited how transformational it was in our journey.

Let's further examine four aspects related to the rise of unreason and our view-point or experience with them in the IT Industry. The four noteworthy aspects are the myth of agility, emergence of nuisance value, creation of complications, and notion of entropy.

Myth of Agility

In the 21st century, the virus of *agility* was injected in IT, and from there it entered into the entire business domain. This virus created an artificial acceleration of the pace of software development very specifically and made it unnatural. In general, the virus of agility causes symptoms of impatience in life.

The concept of agility mainly came from opposing the traditional and well-proven Waterfall model of software development, where each phase is sequential and you cannot move to the next phase before completion of the previous phase. The traditional waterfall model is governed by natural sequential law, where unless you thoroughly complete the design, you do not start development. Like in civil construction, unless you complete plinth you do not start with walls. Agility gurus challenged this sequential and *solid* methodology and introduced parallelism and iterations across all phases of design, development, testing, maintenance, etc., and made it *fluid*. There are some situations where agile methods are suitable, like when the business is not sure of the completeness of their own evolving requirement, but they want to see some implementation to take shape while they work on the rest of the requirements. With the early visibility of the product based on partial requirements, one can then add more features as per new requirements in the next cycle and this process can iterate until all the requirements are implemented. One can ask the question that how come the business is not sure of the requirements in the first place? Well, one reason is the emergence of a plethora of business models which are each unique (as they would like to believe) capturing some potential market opportunity. So, most new-age businesses like start-ups will love agile methods since it frees them from thinking through all the requirements and all the business processes up-front. However, all businesses are not startups so everyone need not go for this unnatural agile methodology. Also, Agile methods introduce great deal of *complications* (in the name of innovation) in daily decision making though stand-up meetings, burn-chart, backlog management, etc. Being over-enthusiastic about demolishing traditions and replacing them with some un-natural approach seems to be a fashionable, forward-looking and modern *outlook*. Many people challenge and break traditions just for the sake of challenging and breaking them.

Emergence of Nuisance Value

Along with the tremendous growth of the IT industry, we have witnessed emergence and expansion of the phenomenon of "Nuisance Value". In addition to the absolute value, things are now also gaining nuisance value. While the absolute value is because of the capability to provide the benefits or advantage, the nuisance value means there is no positive gain but it has value because of the capability of a spoiler. Here are the few examples of how the nuisance value phenomenon is catching up and expanding.

1. Nuisance value of buzzwords- Buzzwords do not add or provide the real knowledge or capability of any subjects or do not simplify any technology either. But if you do not use the buzzwords in your regular business you will be deemed as buffoon, outdated and left behind.

2. Nuisance value of Industry events: Participation in industry events does not provide any ROI in terms of gaining the extra knowledge or business opportunities. But if you do not participate then you will be deemed as laggards and likely to be at a disadvantageous position in the business.

3. Likewise business conferences and participation in ranking related rigmarole may not generate net new business but if you are not participating you are tagged as an adamant *loser*.

4. Nuisance value of software upgrades: Software upgrades that are forced by the vendor provide no useful and visible gain but if you do not upgrade, even the working features will stop working.

5. Nuisance value of technology in Information security: Information security is indeed a matter of business risk management and business should decide the risk management strategy and appetite of taking risk with potential gains. But technology has taken over these matters. Even though technology has no understanding of business, it decides the business risk and security policies. Information security overheads are completely justified on the real and imaginary troubles.

Creating Complications

Making complex (or even simple) things complicated is the example of rising unreason in the business. Software licensing models, legal clause that introduce legal solution for technical problem, are very common examples.

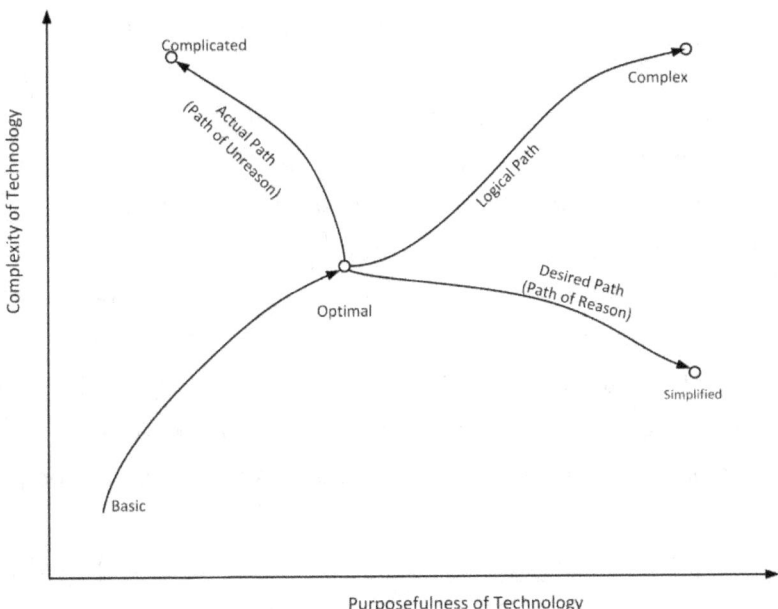

Figure 1: Making complex things complicated is unreasonable.

Complex is different than complicated. Complexity is often essential in the modern world, but complication is the negative, unwanted part of the complexity.

Let's take automobiles as another example to understand complexity and complicatedness in relation to *optimality* of a technology. Cars have been around for over a hundred years now and about 30-40 years back, all car mechanisms were almost standardized. Working of steering, engine, gear-box, differential, brakes, etc. Obviously, there are some variations in each depending on the performance expected and segments like luxury or low-cost etc. But the whole car was more or less a standard machine and it achieved optimal *Price-Performance-Comfort-Safety* ratio around the years 1980-90. After that point of optimality, there have been some more innovations and optimizations in fuel-injection, engine-performance, body-material and weight, safety, and most notably in electronics. These are all great enhancements but incremental none-the-less - with more marketing value and comfort than real need. But it all made the car *reasonably* complex compared to what we had 50 years back. Now we just can't open the hood and fix our cars anymore. Earlier anyone could have opened and fixed a carburetor which worked on a very simple principle of air-suction by engine creating a partial vacuum in the carburetor chamber making it to draw fuel. Now no one dares touch a fuel-injection *system* which is often computer controlled. We have replaced simple parts by complex systems.

And now EVs (Electric Vehicles) have drastically simplified the mechanical parts as there is just a battery and an induction motor. Fuel-injection system is gone for good along with the gear box, transmission, exhaust system, catalytic converter and many more moving parts. But it has added sufficient complexity to the software part including provision of Auto-pilot. Software usually accompanies a legal agreement, disclaimer, etc., that we all are used to signing without reading. But in case of self-driven cars, can we afford to do the same? And the governments will need to amend traffic laws, the moral aspects of decision making has to be looked at, Insurance aspects have to be reexamined (who should be insured – car or car-company?), etc. So, settling an insurance claim arising out of some accident involving a human-driven and self-driving car will be a complicated matter, at least for some years.

But in many situations, we reach optimal technology and then make it complicated due to some vested interests or lack of thinking.

Complicatedness is the unnecessary complexity and occurs when non-value-added parameters are added in any system. Complexity is natural progression, while complication is man-made and enforced. In any business, legal teams in particular, play a very *good* role in making it complicated.

Entropy

In our college physics, we learned about entropy—under the law of thermodynamics. In thermodynamics, entropy is the property that determines the energy available for useful work. We would take this concept of physics and apply it to the service-management domain of IT organizations. So, entropy determines the resources available for *useful* work.

In plain English, *entropy* is defined as the degree of disorder or uncertainty in the system. Typical attributes are chaos, disorganization, and randomness.

The second law of thermodynamics says that the entropy of a system will increase relentlessly if you do not do anything to control it.

We will apply this analogy onto two examples. First to IT, and specifically IT Operations (service management). IT, as we have briefly talked about, is central to businesses mainly because key business processes are modeled and executed on IT systems. Let's take a bank as an example where IT systems corresponds to Servers, Network, Databases, etc., which are procured from some vendor(s) and key business processes like Internet Banking, Trade Settlement, Customer Support, etc., are developed as Application software or bought as package(s) from some vendors. So, an IT system is a fairly complex stack of multiple sub-systems and *running* it as per the user and stakeholder expectations to deliver a *System Performance* is one key objective. A fund-transfer transaction that must be done within a minute, is an example of System Performance. Users and stakeholders, who are humans, have other expectations also, such as help needed if they are stuck while logging-in to the system. Such aspects of running the system come under *Service Performance*. A login/password problems should be fixed within an hour is an example of *Service Performance.*

Due to the effect or law of entropy, *Service Performance* and *System Performance* will degrade automatically within a period of time if we do not take appropriate steps to maintain it. This seems counter-intuitive but true.

Entropy can be caused internally as well as externally. The external entropy is caused by the incompatibility among product vendors and technology that we often see in almost all IT organizations. While each vendor provides the best practice to manage the individual technology, the cross-vendor integration is often inadequate and automatically increases the entropy of the organization. In the zest of acquiring best-of-breed technologies, many organizations have dozens of technologies.

Internal entropy is created by people working with disintegrated processes and focusing on wrong issues. In order to eliminate the negative impact of entropy, we need both technical and service-process management. In other words, a well-designed process will begin with a minimum baseline entropy value and thus establish a system of order in managing the service. However, if you let the process remain static, and you do nothing to make that process dynamically change with the service need, entropy will increase relentlessly. Therefore, process management becomes an imperative need.

Second example pertains to the process of scientific discovery to invention to the technology exploitation of the original science. In the past eras, all this was a steady process with natural pace with adequate control of wisdom in the domain of a small number of wise people. These people had the rationale of comfort and necessity rational of technology which we will discuss in the next chapter of Technology Innovations.

Technology Inventions

I believe in intuitions and inspirations. I sometimes feel that I am right. I do not know that I am.

Albert Einstein

A hallmark of Einstein's career was his use of visualized thought experiments (German: Gedankenexperiment) as a fundamental tool for understanding physical issues and for elucidating his concepts to others. As a child, he imagined riding a beam of light and wondered about the passage of time in such a journey, eventually discovering the theory of special relativity.

When we think of invention and discovery, we think of Einstein, Newton, Edison, and Tesla etc. They were all geniuses who established new frontiers of knowledge and greatly understood many natural phenomena, and gave us technologies like, electricity, light-bulb, LED, atomic energy, atom-bomb etc. Just to mention that LED bulbs and Solar panels that we use these days are based on photovoltaic-effect for which Einstein won the Nobel Prize in 1921. GPS Maps on our mobile-phones or cars without which we cannot think of driving these days, uses Satellites that circle around the Earth for accurately locating position of our vehicle, is also based on Einstein's theory of relativity for correcting time. Tesla's alternating current is a major reason we have electric supply at our household and the Induction motor he invented based on alternating current that drives EVs (Electric Vehicles) now. So fundamental inventions have far-reaching, unforeseen implications reaching into hundreds of years. There can be many more examples in each field of science where far-reaching implications are visible today for innovation that predates fifty, a hundred or even five-hundred years. Fundamental innovations of modern times in semiconductors, computing, communication and Internet are in the same league.

Innovations can be fundamental, transformational, or incremental. Earlier Innovation was the forte of few individual geniuses, but now it is done through organized teams of researchers who work in academia or research labs, and in some large corporations, like IBM, known for their research work. There are still individual brilliances that matter, but it has become teamwork now. Science and scientific community push the frontiers of knowledge resulting in research and publications. Academia and research labs have been the main driving force behind many innovations. Thousands of universities across the world are engaged in research work in their chosen fields and publish a lot of work in journals of repute. Publishing is a hallmark of acceptance of research by the scientific community and acknowledgement that the published work definitely adds to the existing body of knowledge in a significant way. Thus, publishing has become the main benchmark of a researcher, and number of publications per year becomes a yardstick to measure their performance. Another yardstick is how many times a published work or *Paper* is cited by another papers.

This whole phenomenon has been named "publish or perish" by academia and is a well-known fact of life in all universities. If your paper count and reference count to your papers is not adding up, you may not be rewarded or promoted. This also sets fierce competition among teams of researchers working under different guides to push their collective numbers as high as possible. Many research grants that one gets solely depend on such numbers. Of course, there is genuine research happening all the time and many universities, and this phenomenon has worked both in favor and against good research depending upon the ethos of a specific research team. It is a fact that the volume or quantity of research output far exceeds the quality of research, and incremental innovation leading to publishing has become a norm. Like every industry, researchers have also become volume seekers and the mindset for incremental delta improvement is deeply set. After all who wants to perish!

In the corporate world, the desperation to publish papers is replaced by filing of patents. A business would rather file a patent instead of publishing a paper for obvious reasons that a paper once published is a public property while a patent is your corporate asset that can be monetized over a long period of time. So, in corporations the number of patents filed by an individual is the benchmark for measuring individual performances and how the patent gets monetized over a period of time is also an important aspect. Patents are powerful corporate assets hence "patent-or-perish" would be an equivalent notion here and hence one tends to file many patents that are incremental or very clever small process improvement, just to get the numbers. Large and famous businesses file thousands of patents each year but only a few have far-reaching implications.

It has become more a number game and "one-up-man"ship game wherein a corporate can boast of its total number of patents in its portfolio. The pharmaceutical industry is all about patents and they are true patents in the sense that molecules discovered or created are used in medicines. Similarly, there are many "Process patents" owned by companies in chemical, petrochemical, hydrocarbon industries where patents matter a lot.

If we carefully analyze the technological inventions in the history of mankind till today, we shall be inclined to think that (and we believe correctly so) almost all fundamental inventions in technology have happened by the 20th century and it is just refinements and commercialization of those in the 21st century. By fundamental invention, we mean the invention that is original and not derived from the earlier work. Many innovations are also termed as invention, but there is a difference. Every invention is an innovation but every innovation is not an invention.

As an example, in the table below, we have picked up ten of the many hot inventions, deemed to be of the 21st century and shaping the world, and traced their roots to the past century.

No	Technology	Root
1	Artificial Intelligence	John McCarthy coined the term in 1956 although Church-Turing thesis was there from 1943 Expert System in 1980 Proven applications in the late 1990s for logistics, data mining, medical diagnosis and other areas

No	Technology	Root
2	Machine Learning	Term was coined in 1959 by IBM Tested program in 1960 on IBM 704 Artificial Neural Network with Back propagation in 1973
3	Block Chain	Theory established in 1991 Implementation initiated in 1998
4	Social Media	First online social network in 1997 -Six Degree concept was established around the same time
5	Crypto currency	RSA and Public-private Key based fundamental algorithm - 1977 Electronic Money commercialized by DigiCash in 1995
6	Robotics	Simple Robot exhibiting biological behavior in 1948 First Industrial Robot with Six axes 1973
7	GPS	First Prototype in 1978 Full constellation of 24 satellites in 1993 General Theory of Relativity used for time correction by Einstein in 1915
8	IOT	Network of smart devices by CMU in 1982 Ubiquitous computing by Mark Weiser in 1992 MOSFET – the key semiconductor technology for devices in IOT was developed in 1959
9	Mobile OS	Apple's Newton OS for portable devices in 1993 Palm OS in 1996, Symbian OS in 1998
10	Cloud	Time-Sharing OS by IBM and DEC in 1960 Virtual Private Network by Telecom Industry in 1990

So, if the fundamental inventions are rapidly declining then what are the inventions that this century can claim? These are the business model inventions to make money faster and at larger scale by use of technology as depicted in Figure 2.

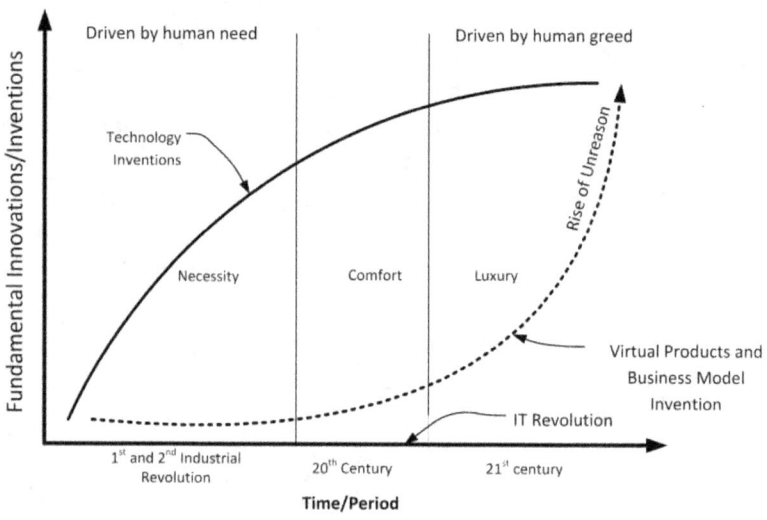

Figure 2: Why are we running out of fundamental technology inventions.

The above figure is self-explanatory and we should be happy that all our necessities and comfort are taken care of largely by technology. Life is relatively easier, standard-of-living is much higher and still rising, life-expectancy is higher that creates the illusion that health is better; though living longer and living healthy are two different things. Also, what is considered to be a luxury today, soon becomes comfort or necessity and thus we keep pushing the bar higher and higher. As said perfectly in Alice and Wonderland:

we keep running faster and faster to remain in the same place !

Why are we running out of fundamental inventions? Aren't there any new fundamental discoveries to be made based on which some unthinkable new technology will emerge for the next hundred years?

Aristarchus was the first person to hold that the Sun rather than the Earth is at the center of the planetary system, that all the planets go around the Sun rather than the Earth. From the size of the Earth's shadow on the Moon during a lunar eclipse, he deduced that the Sun had to be much larger than the Earth, as well as very far away. He may have reasoned that it is absurd for so large a body as the Sun to revolve around so small a body as the Earth. He put the Sun at the center, made the Earth rotate on its axis once a day and orbit the Sun once a year. This all he did 2200 years ago!

Aristarchus and many before and many after him, had no technology, not much science and mathematics apart from Pythagoras and Euclid theorems, and a few basic tools but they discovered Nature and invented great concepts. Today with all the advanced technologies at our fingertips, what do we really discover or invent? Is it the abundance of technology that inhibits our capability for fundamental inventions? Do we get too engrossed in technology itself instead of thinking deeply about fundamental questions? Earlier we had no tools and technologies but abundance of time to think. Now we have an abundance of tools and technologies but no time and no inclination to think.

Things are not getting exciting or our appetite for excitement is now beyond current technologies. More than a dozen years back we had smart-phones and we still have some 10th or 11th version of the same iPhone. Same thing is applicable for cars, entertainment, healthcare, etc. There are occasional discoveries in fields like healthcare and using AI we try to make a splash in some conferences, but they are all still not that kind of fundamental inventions. Self-driving cars can be considered transformational and close to fundamental invention in transportation. But there is no new utility or category that has emerged in the last 15-20 years. Almost everything is firmly set on delta increments.

Looking back, scientific revolution predates Industrial revolution when Europe took the lead in around 1500 AD and science and mathematics became somewhat important. But science and technology were fairly independent of each other. Technologies and innovations existed since discovery of wheel and fire to bullock-carts and fire-arms without any associated science at that time. Artisans like carpenters, masons, ironsmiths, etc., were technologists of that time who created, improved and perfected many technologies of common use at that time. Even today, we find many brainy folks with no formal education but are great innovators for things of everyday utility. With very meager resources, they are able to innovate things that are truly amazing. In India, this kind of innovation is termed as *Jugaad* which is now recognized world over.

But coinciding with the industrial revolution, large businesses as well as governments realized that it pays to invest in science, which then fructifies into technology, which will give them long-term business or military advantage. Aviation, atomic-energy, cryptography, computer science, medical science etc., greatly progressed during world-wars and continues to progress for military and business interests alike. Powerful nations have become much more powerful basically through science and technology and business houses became global conglomerates mainly riding on technology. Not surprisingly most science and technology research work is supported by sizable grants given by government and big business houses. Before the beginning of the scientific revolution around 1500 AD, governments or rulers were mainly sponsoring arts, religion and philosophy etc., and did not pay much attention to science and technology. There were some exceptional rulers and kings who themselves were deeply interested in astronomy and many important scientific and mathematical discoveries were made. But science and mathematics was not a formal discipline and was not given its due importance. Even in warfare -- for almost a thousand years most wars were fought with the same weaponry and largely relying on numerical strength of the army. Now the warfare is completely technology based and man may be completely out of the equation in future wars.

While governments may have deep interest in fundamental science-led innovations that can give them truly unfair advantage and make them mightier, businesses are mainly interested in profits and growth by way of winning more customers and more wallet shares. Thus, businesses exploit the same technology by re-packaging it variously with some incremental improvements and compete on price and after-sales service etc. Understanding customers and markets is more important for businesses than understanding Nature, which is the basis of science.

Of course, some fundamental research goes on in labs like *Cern* on fundamental particles and probably once they even declared finding the elusive God Particle. They do mainly research on finding out (isolating) particles that were present during and immediately after the Big-bang. Incidentally the Internet and HTTP protocol behind the world-wide-web was invented by *Cern* scientist Tim Berners-Lee around the year 1990 as a need to communicate and collaborate on research among scientist community.

So, it really seems all fundamental innovation and scientific discoveries were made by the 20th century and now we are left with some very hard problems pertaining to Big-bang, God, soul, life, death and after-life, etc., which are not of much interest to governments or businesses. Quantum computing may be of interest as probably it will be altogether a new paradigm of computing unlike anything we have seen so far. Elon Musk is trying to go to Mars and settle there, is definitely a path breaking thought rekindling our somewhat lost interest in space-travel. Although there is no, and there will be none anywhere, as beautiful a planet as our mother Earth but it's OK for him to try. His hyperloop and *Boring* like ventures are transformational, if and when they take real shape, but they are again not fundamental inventions. This all is too little an excitement in our society compared to almost 100 years back when Einstein was publishing fundamental discoveries about gravity, light, relativity, etc.

Somehow all great literature, doctrines, philosophies, music, art, political system and political thoughts, etc., were all developed between 15th and 20th century. The golden era of mankind, as they say. Really, there is no more great work in any of these fields. So, plateauing of real inventions and original thoughts is not limited to science and technology, it is all pervasive. This means either there is nothing fundamental left to discover or invent, or our thinking abilities have peaked in the past and are now declining.

In the 21ˢᵗ century, we are firmly in the luxury segment of time-period, where pushing incremental innovation and incremental technologies has become the norm. To ensure sustained consumption, businesses have declared the *consumer as king*. Consumption is projected as a tool for happiness and a consumer rarely thinks that (s)he is getting pleasure but not happiness.

Millions of years ago when Nature made the Earth habitable, it also created the clock that was and is accurate, logical and full of wisdom. This clock has not changed and thus the natural pace of the Earth as created by Nature has not changed. Imagine that the Earth continues to complete its annual journey of over 550 million miles in precisely the same amount of time every year, down to the second-level accuracy for the past millions of years. The Earth also rotates around its axis precisely in the same time every day and has been doing so for millions of years.

Every species including the human race, when came into existence (created by Nature) synchronized their pace of life according to the clock of Nature. Then a significant technology invention came in the form of a timekeeping clock. First artificial (mechanical) clock was invented in the 14th century in Europe and became the standard timekeeping device until the pendulum clock was invented in 1656.

This was the first technology that became instrumental in drifting the human race away from the natural pace of life and became a reference to define the ever-changing pace of human life. All other species continue to follow the natural pace and only the human race went out of sync with natural pace. This was the beginning of abusing the technology. Instead of time keeping, the machine started defining the pace of activities.

Man has been trying to measure time since millions of years. Following the Sun and shadows using a simple stick on the ground, leading to Sun-dials made by great kings where day was divided into equal 8 or 10 parts. But the problem was night, which was one continuous long and dark duration. The work began at sunrise and ended with sunset. There was no great need to keep time and pay as per time spent etc. But with the invention of clocks - that soon became commodities, it was possible for people to divide the work in finer slices and pay as per those slices (per hour labor charges). The advent of electricity and then establishment of factories made working possible during nighttime as well. The combination of clock, electricity, and factories, led to major departure from the natural daylight working to any-time working. The natural biological clock was ignored and people believed and realized that time is the only limited resource which is equally available to everyone, so the greed to use maximum time possible from this 24-hour slot was set-in. Time was considered the most precious and most personal resource which cannot be traded with anyone else, but it can be paid for.

So, clocks, electricity, and factories led to mass-production that changed it all for the humanity. And once you mass-produce; you need mass-consumption so you aggressively promote whatever you made and created artificial craving and created consumers-class. The more you produce and the more you consume, more the economy will grow -- and the richer you will become. This was the main promise of the industrial revolution. Obviously, all this meant trading-off your natural daylight based biological clock, but it was ok since everyone was promised to become rich. Value of time was emphasized by leaders and astute businessmen, that one should not waste a single moment - either you produce something, or consume something in that moment -- that makes the moment worth living, else it is wasted as time is the most perishable entity. That is how we have landed up in manufacturing modern business models.

While time was precious and limited for man, natural resources like minerals, soil, sand, oil, air, water, etc., were taken for granted or considered infinite. Scientific studies reveal that we were consuming natural resources equivalent to one Earth way back in the year 1970 and in 2018 we were consuming natural resources as if we have 1.7 Earths at our disposal. Pollution from factories did bother us for quite some time, as it affected people living nearby those large factories, so awareness and control of pollution became a genuine concern for people and some governments, but we are left with just about 280 Gigatons of Carbon dioxide to be emitted before irreversible climate changes set-in. As per IPCC report (Intergovernmental Panel for Climate Control), we have time only up to the year 2030 before this quota will be over and irreversible changes will set in.

Although there is no fundamental invention taking place, a lot of innovation is happening in the 21st century on business front. Let's take a look at some *Business innovations* in the context of the IT Industry and digital goods.

Business of "Magic Square"

We will try to get a glimpse of innovation in business models as depicted in Figure 2 at the start of this chapter. In the context of the IT industry, we have seen the birth and phenomenal rise of Research and Analyst firms. Some of these firms do consulting work also. They had a humble start about 25-30 years ago and now they are formidable market makers and wheeler-dealers of this industry. Their original business model was a genuine research-based teaching to CIOs on "how to make the right decision". The rise of outsourcing and offshoring was best leveraged by these firms and they became almost self-proclaimed *influencers* without many objecting to it. Through their research reports, these firms basically provide information to the buyers of enterprise technology and IT Services. They provide some look-ahead as to which technology is trending in which industry and what is the general *take* of various clients across geographies on certain emerging technologies and concepts, or challenges in the industry, etc. For this, they conduct some internal research and surveys that are routinely conducted in various geographies.

They all started with a very simple subscription model providing useful research reports on various emerging technologies and trends. It soon became quite popular among the corporate world, especially IT companies and major users of IT in their businesses. They also gave view-points on challenges facing the world and IT opportunities there-of, like Y2K, 9/11, dot-com boom and then dot-com bust, etc. They would back-up their viewpoints by surveys and through analytics or infographics with the data gathered, put-forward many viewpoints. Surveys are typically taken by busy executives or line-managers who are free to provide their answers given their background, intelligence, time-available and keenness, but no one questions the quality of this data. They presented outcomes of these surveys in neat 2X2 charts and unique infographics, which were appealing to clients (IT buyers).

They ranked technology vendors in many innovative ways. This ranking can be re-jigged in several ways. A technology could be top-ranked in some geography for some industries, while some rival technology could be top-ranked for different industries and different sets of parameters. This is a master-stroke, as almost every technology firm could be shown in the top quadrant on certain parameters, or in some geography. All technology firms were their clients – after all. If a client is confused as to which is better technology or who is a better vendor for their IT work, they can always hire the same firm for consulting. They would be happy to do that work unless the client is clever enough to notice a clear conflict of interest. They are also happy (and eager) to consult a technology and IT services company as to how to move up in the ranking for their product or services.

A simple business model of selling good research reports to clients is turned on its head to make money from end-clients, IT Service providers, and technology vendors.

These firms also organize yearly extravaganza conferences, with branded names (usually the firm's name to promote company brand). They present some of their upcoming research work and survey findings in these conferences, which is fine. For IT services and product vendors, the conference participation is almost mandatory but it is not cheap – and if you want to speak from the podium since some of your clients might be in the audience, you have to shell-out substantially more. Everything is monetized. Unlike the great extravaganza of auto shows where car-makers spend a fortune, here the conference organizers make a fortune, not only from the event but also from the enhanced brand equity capitalization in other businesses. Similar types of conferences are discussed in next section as well.

The original theme of genuine research-based teaching on how to make the right decision has become shallow buzzword-based reporting with the teaching of what decision to make. CIOs are also buying that because it is turning out to be a safer decision.

This is the most amazing business model and one of the best innovations. And the best part is, almost everyone knows their game, yet they can't get away from it (see the nuisance value section above). The Chief Marketing Officer earns quite a few brownie points through them through suitable ranking, and thus ensures healthy fee payment and proactive conference participation. Also, many budding folks in the company aspire to attend (at the company cost) these yearly extravaganzas, which are held in some exotic place. All this has become part of the IT Industry now. The yearly budgeting processes of most IT companies includes a permanent upward trending line item called Analyst-Fee, which is a testimony to their clout. This is a classic case of creation of successful business models largely based on rising unreason, or lack of right thinking in the IT industry.

Business of Conferences

This is another case of rise of unreason, although it is not so much a new business model but what is new in this is that the original purpose of learning and collaboration is almost lost and agenda of propaganda has taken the center stage and it is done so systematically that despite knowing that there is no ROI for participants, they still participate . Conferences are held in many industry-bodies and academia. In academia there is a term called *conference circuit*, which means conferences that are connected with some common theme and extending the work of previous conferences etc. But conferences we are dealing with here are a bit different.

The business conferences are held by every major IT vendor yearly or biannually. These are extravaganza of the company showcasing their latest range of products, some under-the-hood explanations of their product, some esoteric use-cases demonstrated by a very young-looking innocent guy, some talk by a futurist etc., ending in a mega song-and-dance show and gala-dinner etc. Well, all this is minimum – there could be many more items of interests that one can imagine and include.

All IT service providers whose clients use the products of this company (IT Vendor), would attend these conferences compulsorily by sponsoring it or paying a premium fee for participation. The actual and potential clients will be coaxed into attending, and they may not pay for participation as they are *guests*. An IT service provider is encouraged and ranked based on how many actual and potential clients came through him to attend the conference. IT service providers typically set-up a stall in a cubicle whose size depends on the level of sponsorship. There are Bronze, Silver, Gold, Platinum sponsorships, and one can invent more precious metals if more tiers are needed. So, fundamentally the extravaganza is paid by the IT product and service provider with the hope that visitors coming to their stall will like their service offerings around the product.

The real take-away from these conferences are the contact-list of visitors who came to their stall. Some of these visitors are considered to be potential clients, but many of them are casual visitors, competitors snooping on your offerings, conference hobbyists, etc. The potential clients also visit all other stalls, but everyone thinks their contact-list is unique and hence their conversion ratio will be at least 80%. Some even include this in their yearly budget forecast of additional revenue through conference participation in spite of finding that nothing of this sort materialized in the past 10 years. But human beings, particularly sales folks, are very optimistic fellows who never see any negativity about such things. Every year they put up the stall with the same zeal, same commitment, same expectations, and sometimes same potential clients show up on their stalls - year after year. They also convince some good fellows in their own company to come and make some presentations since they have signed-up for a Gold sponsor which includes one conference presentation. And who attends these presentations? Mainly the people from the same company and some competitors perhaps.

That's why we claim that unreason is rising year-on-year and faster than before that makes conferences in most cases a necessary evil.

Virtual Products and Business Models

Business models, as mentioned, are inventions of the 21st century. Not that they did not exist before as they are essential for any business to position its value-proposition for customers and provide a profit-formula for itself. But their exponential growth in the Internet era is unprecedented.

Take financial markets for instance. There are tens of thousands of mutual funds that carry some mix of stocks from a total stock portfolio of only a few thousands of stocks. Mathematically from a thousand stocks, one can create probably billions of mutual fund portfolios using permutations and combinations. Each mutual fund is a *Unique Product* with little variation based on multiple parameters: industry or sector, risk-appetite, duration, company sizes, etc. And a new parameter can always be invented – just by some thought or idea. And technology (Internet, analytics, Excel) has made it fairly easy now to pick a right set of stocks to carve out a new Product based on some criteria.

Like mutual funds, there are other sets of financial products based on derivatives, hedging, foreign currency, home loans, etc. And home-loan is of particular interest to remind ourselves of the subprime crisis of 2008. That crisis was mainly from failure of a business model that was based on packaging and repackaging of home-loans and associated homebuyers into some sort of security that was traded, re-packaged and re-sold. Obviously, greed and stupidity were the basis of this crisis. Regulators wake up after an event and do the needful, but they cannot intervene in the Invention process of new business models in a capitalist society.

Insurance industry also is witnessing a huge explosion of products. Similar to financial markets, the insurance industry also has invented many products by rehashing and repackaging the same basic old ideas. While every category like, home, car, life, health and projects etc., do need insurance cover but with hundreds of insurance companies each offering hundreds of products in each of these categories is bewildering. Simplicity and minimalistic approach seem to be a thing of distant past. Paradox of choice seems to be a norm in everything.

And then big business models exist on Leveraged Buyouts (LBOs) where Blackstone made a mark as a premium Private Equity firm across the world. Taking a public company private, sprucing it up sufficiently, and then reselling it or going public again was probably a well thought-through model. It certainly was a new business model that came around 1985. It may have existed earlier but Stephen Swarzman of Blackstone gave it brand and fame, and made huge amount of money for its investors and has a market worth of over $600 Billion these days. His fabled story narrated in his book "What it Takes" talks about many key principles of business. Asset restructuring company (ARC) is also a somewhat similar model, which applies to stressed assets mainly and is a fairly innovative model.

Each startup is basically a unique business model that tries to propose some new idea, new value-proposition, new customer base, etc. Startups were there in 1980s also, but the exponential growth in sheer number of startups in this century is noted by everyone. In a city like Bengaluru, which was famous for offshore work on IT services, there are probably ten thousand startups. Extrapolating this across India and other countries like USA, Israel,

South Korea, China, Japan, UK, etc., there may be a million startups. Starting from say a few thousand about 30 years back, this is certainly exponential growth of this century. The number of students in MBA schools and growth of MBA schools itself is one leading indicator of potential startups in time to come.

We can appreciate this is the age of exponential rise of Virtual Products and Business models. We can find many more examples in other industries like Music, Entertainment, Media, Travel, Hospitality, etc. Most business models deal with virtual or Digital goods. Mutual funds, insurance products, financial products, LBO, ARC, and 90% of startups deal in digital goods. So, IT and the Internet are the foundations of exponential growth of Business Models of the 21st century.

Limitations of Technology

"It has become appallingly obvious that our technology has exceeded our humanity."

— Albert Einstein

Unfortunately, exceeding humanity is a negative attribute and matter of limitation that it cannot keep the goal of humanity in its so-called progress. Technology is the commercialization of science. Science is knowledge but technology is not absolute knowledge. Initially we wanted to title this chapter as poverty of technology but after some thinking, poverty seemed much stronger word to us. It is like hate – you may dislike something but that does not mean you may hate that thing. Likewise, poverty is not an inherent property of technology. Technology is rich and rich can also have limitations. It is the limitation and mankind has exposed the limitation as the poverty by the way of applying the technology where it should not be applied.

Technology does not produce wisdom, though it helps in producing knowledge and sharing as well as distributing knowledge. This is among the big limitations of the technology and we will elaborate on it more in the later chapter when we discuss wisdom.

Limitation of technology on producing wisdom is due to another limitation: machines cannot think, though they can compute fast on enormous amounts of data and give the illusion of thinking.

Technology does not produce happiness though it has capability to deliver pleasures - and there is a huge difference between pleasure and happiness. Mankind has been blessed with the ability to obtain real happiness that works at the level of wisdom. Pleasures are obtained by the instant gratification of senses and do not require a person to be wise. For example, food and sex are the most primitive elements to derive pleasure that are available to all creatures in Nature.

Technology does not produce health, though it helps to stay alive for a longer time. True health is the quality of the body that keeps you free from illness and is natural by design. The self-healing design of the human body is amazing. It is natural design, and technology, whatsoever may be the advancement, will always have limitations to match that. We are abusing this by junk food and unnatural lifestyle and deteriorating it, and then using technology to keep it alive, not healthy. There is a lot of difference between staying alive and staying healthy. Design of Nature does not sustain unhealthy beyond a point where mankind is using technology to sustain it for the purpose of business. On the other hand, Nature has very strict - or shall we say time-tested processes on trading off between healthy life and lengthy life that may look cruel at individual level. But Nature has a track record of a billion year compared to modern technology which is around for only a couple of hundred years.

Our parents did not have refrigerators so we could not preserve food. In our home, we cooked every day two times and ate because of inability to store in a refrigerator. So, we ate fresh food every day, every time. Technology has given us refrigerators that help us to avoid eating fresh food. In fact, our parents had much less technology but they were eating organic food, they were eating fresh food and they were breathing clean air and drinking much cleaner water. In general, the lifestyle they had is now not affordable by common man today. Thanks to technology !

Every year around summer, we are blessed to have sunbirds making a nest in our little balcony. We witness their nest-making process then laying eggs and nurturing their kids for about 5-6 weeks as keen observers. It is a very exciting and joyful time for us when we see life taking shape from such close quarters. We are really indebted to sunbirds that they choose our balcony as their home for such a beautiful natural event of child-birth. We were very sad when one of the bird kids died in the nest, while the other sibling came out chirping. Being humans, we are very worried about how the lone little sun-bird would survive all by himself. Being humans, we do not have complete faith in Nature. We are still pondering over a lot of "what-if" scenarios as to what we could have done differently to ensure survival and safety of little sunbirds.

And here is the ultimate limitation of technology that it can not create *Life*. You need life to create life. Many lab experiments seem to *produce* life but actually they do not. The seed of life has to come from another life and then one can fertilize and do many other things in a lab.

When our little sunbird kid died, we knew that no amount of science and technology or money could bring him back to life, but even Nature could not inject back life once taken. And fortunately, or unfortunately, science and technology have stopped looking into matters pertaining to life and death. It has come to terms with its own limitations in these matters. Most other limitations that we have discussed above, like happiness, health, wisdom are connected with thinking and only a life form can think because thinking requires intention and feeling which is a privilege of life-forms only. Artificial creation of any sophistication will never have these characteristics due to lack of life.

Let's get into some lighter, sportier and practical matters now.

Collaboration and Teamwork.

Most of the progress of mankind can be attributed to some great individual geniuses in the past but collaboration and teamwork has also played an important role. But humans are not naturally designed to collaborate and work in teams, while they may excel individually. Unlike ants, and bees, we are non-team species. One can always wonder at the way ants accomplish a complex task (for them) to move a large dead cockroach through a complex (uneven) territory for their height and visibility. But they have very simple protocol (rules of communication) and probably with some trial-and-error, they accomplish such tasks near optimally. Same is true for bees. How the queen bee rules and how they collect and deposit honey and organize themselves to defend the queen and themselves, are examples of great and natural "in-born" teamwork. New members are not *taught* to be team players, and I suppose no pep-talk is given about *team-spirit, winning, killer-instinct,* etc. But they all accomplish great team work routinely as part of everyday life. One can call it the power of Nature.

Sports like soccer or hockey combine individual brilliance and teamwork superbly and the great teams have both factors in their favor but their ratio is changing. In hockey, where India has reigned supreme from 1930 to perhaps 1960 winning seven Olympic gold medals, including the most famous one in the 1936 Berlin Olympic where Hitler himself was present in the stadium at the final between Germany and India. India won that match with supreme ease mainly due to legendary wizard Dhyanchand. Of course, the entire Indian team played very well and many goals were scored, but everyone was mesmerized by Dhyanchand's artistry. The ball would simply stick to his hockey-stick and he would pierce through any number of opposite team players no matter how they came together to snatch the ball away from him. Someone accused him of using some sort of adhesive on his hockey stick so that the ball sticks to it while he dribbles it. To a naked eye, it actually seemed to stick to his hockey-stick while he was dribbling around in zig-zag manner at crazy speeds ducking the opposition. But it was obviously not the case and investigation found no substance in the allegation. Dhyanchand was known to practice for long hours all by himself and sometimes with his brother who was also a great player himself, dribbling the ball on railway tracks with a surgical precision not allowing the ball to fall off the narrow slippery track for long distances. With India's thumping win, even Hitler rose from his seat along with the entire stadium to a round of thunderous applause. A statue of Dhyanchand was erected in Berlin to remember such a great player.

Contrast that with Hockey today, where no player keeps the ball for more than 2-3 seconds and makes long-passes to teammates. It is all a hit and run game now. The game has changed from individual brilliance to teamwork. Nowadays, the team spends months together in camps practicing together so as to bond as a team. Individual brilliance has definitely taken a back seat compared to fitness and teamwork. I recently witnessed a hockey match where Indian team was playing Australia. Indian players were keeping the ball in possession for much longer than needed and not passing the ball to the most appropriate player who was positioned to score. I almost counted a dozen occasions where Indian players were just dribbling the ball and losing the possession but they did not pass. So, Indian team neither had Individual brilliance nor team play. Australia had almost the same level of players Individually but they passed the ball with *unselfish* ease and that made the whole difference. Why was teamwork lacking in Indian team? Was it lack of training? Or was it something deeper? I feel our selfishness comes greatly in the way of teamwork. Each player wants to make a difference and wants to be seen making the difference and scoring the goals all by himself. So, all the training is blurred the moment he gets the ball and sees himself as scoring the goal and in this state of mind all his own teammates are lost from his vision. He sees only opposition players and tries to dribble his way through them – in Dhyanchand style. But he is no Dhyanchand, so within no time, he is outsmarted and the ball is snatched away. I am using Indian team as an example here, but many team games involving the best of the teams suffer

this fate in many crucial games. The best performing team with regards to team-game, falters in the finals due to lack of team spirit. Our human instinct to be selfish takes over our artificially acquired sense of teamwork.
There was another well-known story, which indirectly relates to teamwork or camaraderie.

A king who was proud of the honesty and team-spirit of his citizens was challenged to fill a big pond in the center of his capital city by a glass of milk poured into it by each citizen during a dark night. The pond was emptied of its water and kept ready for receiving milk one night. Next day morning, to the King's and everyone's astonishment, the pond was filled with pure water. Every citizen thought all others were going to pour milk into the pond, so their one glass full of water instead of milk would not make any difference – and no one will anyway come to know of their pouring water instead of milk in the dark night. They also further convinced themselves that they were not doing anything wrong since they would rather feed this milk to their kids instead of wasting it. To extend the story, the next day the King again emptied the pond and put a video camera (which could be a decoy) – and to no one's surprise, next morning the pond was full with pure white milk.

Under strict observance, punitive measures, etc., one can act to be part of a team, but given a little freedom, we act in our selfish interest and credit seeking ways on the first opportunity.
Related to our IT Industry experience, many capabilities or resources were duplicated by each region, resulting in lower

overall profit, and unnecessary competition or ill-will within the company. So, some sort of incentive scheme was floated at leadership level, which made it mandatory to help the other team with your unique or unused capabilities, special domain knowledge etc. It was not a perfect scheme but a good start, and many tweaks were made with learning from each real situation. A "collaboration Index" was designed which indicated some sort of ratio of the business you do and business you enable other teams to do. But even after a year or so, while the collaboration index showed some upward trend, the real spirit of collaboration was nowhere to be seen. People collaborated to be compliant and to place it on record and get the due credit, or avoid the penalty for not collaborating, but nothing beyond that. Intent was not to really collaborate but to create the evidence of collaboration in the measurement system. Similarly, In IT security this tendency is very common where the intent is to pass the security audit rather than actually having the security in place.

Humans, who are anyway left with very few natural instincts, have no such natural instinct for teamwork so they have used their intelligence and thinking capabilities to come up with many ways and means to accomplish teamwork based on the situation at hand. For military-like situations, command-and-control structure is preferred. Democracy is also supposed to be a form of teamwork. Playing most competitive games is another kind of teamwork. And writing large complex software is yet another. But all these are artificial in the sense that one has to be trained in a particular type of teamwork. If you are a great team player as a footballer, you may not transfer those skills of teamwork to software development. Teamwork has to be managed very tactfully, as humans are emotional and political creatures. This basically boils down to the fact that teamwork in humans is not natural and is very expensive. We spend a huge amount of effort and resources in managing the team and teamwork, sometimes so much, that efforts for managing the work exceed the actual work (output). If one carefully examines hierarchy in a large corporation, only the bottom most layer is really the working layer responsible for output - all layers above are basically managing the team below it. A perfectly flat organization, like that of bees or ants, would have a queen bee CEO at the top and rest all workers - no middle layers.

In a distributed computing environment, we have a term called "Compute-Communication ratio". A large and complex task is subdivided into many smaller tasks such that the final result can be aggregated by combining results from all tasks. Each sub-task is executed on a separate computer called a Node. A Node has to accomplish the assigned task and communicate the result to other Nodes who then can accomplish their piece of work, there is a great deal of communication involved which does not really add any value to the main job of computing. So, if we are spending more effort communicating compared to computing, we are in a disadvantaged situation. It also means that adding more Nodes to the existing network of Nodes will get only marginally more computing power. Law of diminishing returns kicks-in for every system after a certain critical number in a given configuration. In case of distributed computing, this ratio can be measured, which helps in designing optimal topology of Nodes. Likewise, in a human based team also, this law of diminishing return sets in at some size or complexity, resulting in *complications* and wasted efforts.

Now let's turn to technology and ask ourselves whether technology has helped solve the problem of teamwork among humans. With a plethora of technologies at the command of a finger, one can reach anyone across the world in an instant. One can talk or have a video call or have a team meeting with several members across different countries, and more such things virtually free or at a very low cost. Just 30 years back, all this would have been a distant dream, is now a cheap commodity. Communication is supposed to be the biggest facilitator of team building and team working is well known. So, have human teams become better by at least an order of magnitude as communication and collaboration technologies become several orders of magnitude better and affordable? We all know the answer, which is a distinct no! While there have been some improvements and lesser things are falling through the proverbial crack, but that has not made a significant dent in our lack of natural instinct for teamwork. Mission Moon of NASA was an example of great team-work that sent man to the moon and brought it back in 1969 when none of the technology-based collaboration and communication tools existed. Would it have made a difference if the same mission is repeated today? Probably to some extent - but would not be a ten- or hundred-fold improvement.

Technology has contributed significantly in many areas and affordable communications has very significantly changed our lives and standards of living. In the corporate world that needs great teamwork, technology has provided many tools for Collaboration and Project Management, for scheduling physical and virtual meetings, etc. We have many tools for analyzing performance of our team or opposition in games like Soccer or Cricket to attack on weaknesses and play to our strength etc. Technology has changed many games like Cricket where accurate rendering of the trajectory of the ball can be drawn to decide LBW, and whether a ball touched the rope for a Six.

We love tools to ease work since the invention of the wheel, so nothing wrong with technology providing many tools. Tools extend our reach and make our senses more powerful in some way. But can tools replace our instincts, or lack of it? Humans have a lot of flaws, individually, and collectively even more. So, trying to cover up those by technology is not exactly working out.

The fundamental reason for many of these limitations is that Technology cannot think.

Does Technology Make People Dumb?

As technology gets complex to deal with complex problems, the abstraction layer that is exposed to users masks many things that a person needs to know otherwise. However, in most cases the user just sees the miracle that happens but remains ignorant on how the miracle happens with the help of technology. Although it is good in many cases as it is exactly the purpose- hide the complex stuff and present the simple method to use. Also, ignorance about how technology works is not a problem. The problem occurs when people do not learn the basics. For example, the availability of calculators should not eliminate the need and ability to learn the basic arithmetic. Before the point of sale system (POS) was introduced in retail shops, shopkeepers were doing the basic arithmetic easily. Today, if the POS system is down, the business halts. Writing skills among the kids are vanishing and giving ways to finger skills on keyboards and phones. Individuality is lost, which used to be the identifier of each kid's work in the form of handwriting. Now we are seeing even the keyboards getting optional with the rise of voice commands.

The contrasting phenomenon is that technology unmasks many things that most people do not need to know most of. Software technology has exposed many parts of the digital products to the users with the expectation that the user is smart to use. In the initial stage it challenges the smartness of user and then make him dumb. For example, many skilled and experienced drivers find it difficult to drive new generation cars because of overwhelming software controls. Car dealers in the US now have an additional job of trainers to teach buyers to use features and functions. The primary skill of safe driving goes in the background and you are judged not on the core driving skill but on the software user skills. Nicholas Carr in his book "Does IT Matter" has raised the question – Is IT irrelevant? And stated, "Our intelligence is withering as we become dependent on artificial variety. Rather than lifting us up, smart software seems to be dumbing us down"

Technology makes people dumb because it imposes the habit of "not thinking". It takes away the natural instinct of using the senses – how much to eat, whether to feel hot or cold. Technology makes them Dumb as well as dependent. It is also addictive which further aids the dumbness. It also puts the smart or intelligent people, and not so smart and not so intelligent people in the same bracket as both groups can do the same tasks using common technologies.

All of us were fascinated with emails and saw its great utility in our work initially and then in personal life as well. Sending and receiving greetings like wishing birthday or New Year through email was a novelty, which we all loved before the dawn of the 21st century. But soon, email was integrated with the calendar and then you could write little macros or programs that could automatically fetch birthdays and email addresses from your contacts and send greetings. This ensured you never missed greeting someone on his or her birthday. It helped you organize this important aspect of your life. Upon receiving such email greetings, you would graciously thank the sender via email. Soon enough, you realized that replying to such greetings could be automated too. So, it is your machine, which sends a birthday wish to your loved one, and his or her machine responds with thanks to your greeting. You or your loved one need not be aware, and need not be in the loop while respective machines are doing it.

Computers are great machines to organize things and greatly aid human memory. We are forgetful and sometimes due to stress or many other reasons, cannot remember important things including birthdays. So, using computers to prompt you on some important event is a good idea. But getting over-excited with technology and over-automating personal stuff is stupidity. If people come to know that you have automated sending and receiving all birthday greetings, they will not take your compliments sincerely and they will also think of you to be a superficial person. Human beings are creatures with feelings and automation beyond a point kills all feelings.

We are increasingly depending on navigation provided by the GPS and Maps in our cars. It is definitely one of the greatest conveniences that we are enjoying and it has eased a lot of hard-work of finding a new place which involved looking at a paper-map while driving, asking directions at gas-stations, etc. Now with the online maps and vocal turn-by-turn directions, we are never worried to drive to any unknown location. Availability of these maps spawned new industry segments like Uber and Ola where millions are people are now driving passengers around with consummate ease. Just a few years back, Black cab drivers of

London were very famous for knowing all lanes and by-lanes, each nook-and-corner of London and they would navigate by shortest and good route with their amazing driving efficiency and skills. They had developed a sort of sixth sense about traffic conditions and were well-versed with any detours and diversions, etc. It was an amazing experience to chat with those drivers while riding with them. A detailed study found that due to their memorizing and recalling vast map related information and their passion for driving, their brain scans were different from a normal person. Their whole mind or persona was integrated with their car and the city. In Mumbai, we have Black-and-Yellow cabs. Their drivers also exhibit similar knowledge about Mumbai but London Black-cabs are a league apart.

These days they also use GPS-Maps when required, but imagine if some day the GPS is down for whatever reason. In such a situation, most Ola and Uber drivers would be simply sitting in their cars without any business but these Black-cabs drivers would continue as usual. We have all seen drivers who are clueless about the place, have poor driving and navigation skills and used little or no common sense in locating a place by just looking out. Complete dependence on technology makes them look actually dumb and disconnected.

The point here is, soon we become so dependent on a good technology, like calculators, computers and now GPS Maps, that if they are not available for some reason, our work or business comes to a halt. Over a period of time, our natural instinct to drive around and find a place, sometimes by mere hunch, has substantially reduced and might vanish in some time. Good driving is an intelligent social activity and although we are getting closer to self-driving cars, there will be people who are passionate about driving and will not give-up this joy. Becoming passionate about technology is also fine but using a technology without having any curiosity and not appreciating and knowing some of its fundamentals, is surely not a smart way to live in this age of technology. Unfortunately, majorities are in this category.

A very important aspect of Technology is it saves time for us. Most automation achieved through technology is aimed at saving time and effort. We certainly can accomplish much more in the same 24 hours than our predecessors did. But the question is what do we do in the time that is saved? For most people, the saved time is consumed back by the technology itself in the form of social media and conventional media. Hardly few invest this time in meaningful ways that enhance their thinking capabilities leading to increased wisdom. Technology is so engrossing and enticing to kill the excess time at hand now, that other pursuits have ceased to appeal. In fact, you try hard to save time to kill it and technology is a great help either way.

There is a little childhood story that might make you chuckle a bit.

Once a king was worried about his citizens that they had too much idle time. So, he decides to go around in disguise and check it out first hand. He went to a nearby village and met a person who was counting grains of wheat. Upon asking the person said there were 20 large bags of wheat grains he was counting each grain to ensure they get divided equally in two sets of 10 bags. Aghast by the time-killing approach, the king moved on and met another guy who was taking out a spoonful of water from a large pond and purring into an empty ground. Upon querying he said he was trying to measure the pond capacity in number of spoons. After going further, the king met another man who was climbing up and down trees and counting all leaves on each tree. By now the king was sufficiently irritated so could not resist and asked why you guys in this village are all doing such stupid time-wasting things. 'Oh, you should meet our king who is doing most stupid time-wasting thing' the leaf counting man replied. The king was surprised and asked what the king was doing? Upon which the man said the king was killing his idleness by going round in disguise to witness what other idle people were doing.

Where Technology is Taking Us?

A calm and modest life brings more happiness than the pursuit of success combined with constant restlessness
Albert Einstein

The ultimate aim of life is to achieve the maximum satisfaction and happiness and that is possible only by optimizing (minimizing) wants. Technology is mostly working to deliver what a person *wants* but in reality, *wants* increase significantly faster than technology can deliver. Is technology taking us to the path of happiness? We are inclined to think that technology is diverting mankind from the true goal and purpose of life.

Happiness ought to be the purpose of life and technology has huge potential to deliver that but in all practical matters, technology is more aiming at delivery of instant gratification and pleasures.
Amassing immense knowledge is the means of obtaining wisdom. However, technology is stopping at amassing immense knowledge but cannot take us to the path of wisdom. All that knowledge is used to amass wealth but not towards using the acquired wealth wisely. Gaining and using are two different things (*pana aur bhogana* in Indian philosophy) – so gaining the knowledge or gaining the wealth is different from using the knowledge and

wealth wisely. Mankind can learn this concept from Nature. We love trees because they produce oxygen for us. Right from the state of being a small plant to a full-grown tree, it keeps on producing the oxygen and eventually it dies, leaving behind the deadwood. If you burn that wood (or completely oxidize it by any other process) the amount of oxygen that it would consume is exactly equal to the amount of oxygen that it has produced in its lifetime. The message of Nature is very clear – consume only what you can contribute to Nature. Mankind has not even noticed this law, and whomsoever noticed - even they have blatantly broken this natural law.

Technology is just a tool to make a living and keep the Industry alive. It is also taking us to the path of expanding employment opportunities and money-making opportunities. Since more and more are making their living on technology, more people have vested interest to glorify technology.

Even if not exploiting the technology for employment or money-making opportunities, more and more people are getting obsessed with technology as buyers and take help of technology in every decision whether it makes sense or not. For example, people are using the health application on their mobile device and looking at the data they decide if they are tired or they can work more. It is like deciding to feel hot or cold after looking at the weather forecast or decide how much to eat based on the measurement by health application. Technology is equally available to evil designers as well as to the agencies controlling evil designs.

Looks like we are having excess of technology and that is coming at you at a faster pace. Whatever piece of technology you have, is already obsolete and you know it almost at the time of buying. So you are mentally never committed to that great car you purchased or latest mobile phone or latest laptop, because you know this will last a year or two and the same company will come out with newer models with better looks, or some underlying technology will change like 4G to 5G. We never sign-up for long-term use, and hence we never attempt to understand the basics of great technology that is at your disposal. And this becomes a mindset - you never get involved with the science or technology of the product and simply care for its feature, price, brand and exchange-value, and may be some buzzwords associated with it. And makers of these products also ensure you have least learning time to get going at it. Standardization of some aspects of technology, like user-interface, has made it even simpler to switch among products like phones, cars, and TVs etc.

Technology has also become cheaper, much cheaper, compared to the past. Earlier purchasing a car required your life-time savings perhaps, but now it is merely a monthly EMI afforded by most working and earning persons. Affordability also reduces value and additionally or along with it, results in loss of thinking about basics and that has led to de-linking technology with wisdom, which was earlier linked due to deeper love of technology and not mere temporary fascination. Earlier days, once you owned a piece of technology, say a car, you would think of cherishing it for a life-time and hence would try to understand all aspects of car mechanics and would not mind getting under the hood on every opportunity. And now is the time of excess of everything and excess of affordable technologies, and there is no time and no inclination to know it deeply. Why spend time knowing and getting attached to it if it is going to change soon? And it is cheap or very affordable, so we can throw it away if we do not like it or it stops working for some reason. We will rarely try to fix it unless it is very expensive. And the concept of fixing itself has completely transformed, for good or bad, I do not know. Now, we do not identify and replace a small faulty part, we replace the whole unit containing that part. Recently my steering wheel of car was making some squeaking noise and since my car was under warranty, they replaced the whole steering wheel unit including rack-and-pinion arrangement and steering column etc. I was shocked to know that and felt very sad that they would have trashed all good and working parts as they could not find time or had no inclination or no skill in identifying a small faulty part like a squeaking rubber gasket. Car makers also make their cars such that it has become very difficult to get down to a part-level fixing and their training of maintenance staff also has thus made them mere module or unit-replacement guys instead of developing true understanding of all aspects of working of a car. Same is true for refrigerators, washing machines, TVs and all that. The skill to fix a thing by deeper understanding is not required, not taught, and hence not appreciated. All this means less of thinking, less of analytical skills.

Technology was a little child during the previous generation of baby boomers. It used to be at our command. Be it Car, TV, or Radio, our parents would control it. Now technology is an Adult and seems to have a mind of its own. You cannot control all technologies now and, in many cases, it controls you. Many examples, including Alexa, Driverless or Advanced Electric cars, Auto-piloted planes, and many more, where we are given an illusion of control but it is the technology that is firmly in control. In fact, regarding Auto-pilot planes, which most long-distance planes are, are so designed that a Human being is not supposed to touch any control and simply watch it and press some button in some extreme emergency. Even that function is not really needed to be done by Humans but Technology was little kind to let humans be still in the loop. In many cases, humans can be out of the loop and many large Systems can, and do, run without us. There was a famous cartoon where a Man is guarding a large fully automatic and technologically advanced vault of a bank, and a little dog by the side of the man, is *manning* the man to ensure the man does not touch any control.

There is a great deal of talk on controlling Technology through regulations. In the field of AI and Machine learning, for example, several current tech leaders of Tesla, Facebook, Alibaba, Google, etc., have given their views. But frankly they are tentative about it as they do not know where it could lead, and their main business is based on technology advances so they can not oppose it as such. Almost fifty years back, Isaac Asimov gave famous three laws of Robotics and wrote several stories as to how Robots resolve several conflicts in their own working with humans by using these three simple laws embedded in their brain circuits. Nowadays people also talk about decision making by Driverless cars in situations where they have to make a choice about someone to kill - an old person or a kid. This is also classical *triage* commonly invoked in hospitals where number of patients are more than available resources and Doctors have to take a call whom to save and whom to let go. Like, in the ongoing Coronavirus crisis in India (and many affected countries), the number of ventilators may not be adequate and soon doctors might face the dilemma of whether to put patient A or patient B on a ventilator. They will take a call usually in favour of younger patients who have more life to live. Sounds cruel but that's what triage is - which medical professionals practiced since World War I. Now if there is an Algorithm or AI based system for triage, where this decision is made by a non-human, *unfeeling* technology, would you be comfortable? Trading stocks using algorithms is one thing but deciding on who lives and who dies is altogether a different matter. And, may be, or suppose, the AI based triage systems makes a better but non-transparent decision, would you be OK with it? The decision that the AI systems made, may involve machine learning, some common rules, some context etc., but it will be extremely difficult to convey it to us humans who might think that machine is simply randomizing and probably unjust. But maybe it is good as there is no human doctor to blame about why he or she made a choice in favor of some patient allowing the other to die.

And now there is a talk of infinite connectivity in all spectrums of our lives – whether at home, at office, on roads, anywhere. This is the ultimate dream of the ultimate Smart cities where all homes, utilities, offices, buildings, roads, cars, etc., are all intricately and intimately connected to one another. To realize and implement ultimate connected Life, we seem to need much more connectivity than simple 4G and WiFi. To realize and implement autonomous driving where all cars are in constant communication with all other cars and other objects, we need something more than 4G. The short answer to many such desperate needs to have infinite connectivity is 5G. We had 2G, 3G and now 4G which along with Fiber with regular speeds of 200MB/Sec is already with us. We have enough cell-phone towers all around us and enough underground and overhead cables carrying all the Bits at the speed of light. But 5G is a completely different beast it seems. Every 100 meters, it will need a powerful microwave tower (antenna), which will create a very dense grid of millions of towers all around us. In a city like Mumbai, it will need over hundred thousand such towers, all emitting high-powered microwave radiations. It will be an ocean of Antennas and Tsunami of Radiation. We are no experts in whether it is harmful to human health or not, but do we need all that massive dose of radiation and gigantic infrastructure just to fulfill the promised dream of IoT (Internet of Things) and Smart city? IoT is very good and many implementations already exist which use 4G, WiFi, Bluetooth etc., and create a good enough network for a given situation. Autonomous cars are doing all right on the technology front but there are other challenges there. But we are aiming for a so-called perfect (but absolutely artificial) world with 5G all over the planet, whether we need it or not. 4G and Fiber are quite recent and deliver very good performance for all office and home needs. Their full potential is yet to be fully tapped. All those infrastructures of 4G will become outdated and junked with 5G. What a colossal waste !

I am told Wuhan was the first city where 5G was implemented. Not sure how to read further into it at this juncture. As mentioned earlier, humans are anyway disconnected from Nature so perhaps massive doses of radiation have no effect on human beings, as claimed by 5G technology companies. But it has been found that the radiation of the 5G grade, causes severe health issues in birds, fishes, etc. But we will overlook this also along with other environmental warnings related to greenhouse gas emissions, etc., as we are used to overlooking or ignoring such warnings.

Let's keep aside health hazards as wolf-cry for the time being. But 5G is sure to create unprecedented surveillance possibilities where every movement of everything can be monitored. So 5G is of immense interest to the governments as well as to the big business houses. They are surely going to make consumers The King !

All these provide a glimpse of things to come, and some are already happening, where humans are still in command. But soon the control may not be with humans and Skynet like possibilities cannot be ruled out. And after a while, humans may not be competent enough to be in the command as they would have considerably lost their thinking abilities and due to increasing dependence on technology, they would easily yield to be subservient to technology.

Since most of the technology is related to communication, let's understand some situations where explicit communication does not matter. About 20 years ago one of the authors went for a *Vipassana* course which was group meditation for 11 days during which no one talks to anyone for anything. You sit and meditate for long hours since very early morning in large groups, go for breakfast, lunch and tea at predefined hours in a cafeteria. There are hundreds of people in the cafeteria serving themselves but there is no human chatter – only little noise of utensils. Nothing is verbally explained about where to take utensils from and where to keep it back, or what to do if some food item is over, or you spilled something by mistake, etc. You just observe, sometimes wait in silence, get your stuff and move on. If you don't get what you were waiting for, then also you just move on. No protocol is explained to you beforehand but almost everyone gets it right by the second day. The kitchen which is attached to the cafeteria is also virtually noiseless where mass cooking goes on with many cooks and workers constantly moving around, but no human chatter there also. The entire life for 11 days is managed without uttering a single word while there are hundreds of people around you in meditation sessions, evening discourses, cafeteria, etc. Initially you feel extremely restless but soon you are surprised at this wonderful sight and experience. You realize how futile it is to talk and how we spend our precious mental energy in talking, showing urgency, assuming self-entitlement, etc. Little observation, some wait, some patience, little eye-contact is all you need for most collaborative work. A calm descends upon you and you feel really rested. It does not mean you are relaxing or lazing around, as there are tough meditation sessions and there is routine work to be. You also tend to curtail your needs automatically and don't demand things from yourself to be perfectly dressed or perfectly shaven.

Another magical thing you realize during these 11 days is you do not need any media in your life. There are no newspapers, no TVs, no mobile phones allowed to be carried with you so no social media, etc. So, you are really cut-off from the world. Initially you are very much worried as to how the world will carry on without you keeping track of it by your mere act of reading the newspaper or watching TV. How would you handle some emergencies in case someone needs you or you need someone? But all those imaginations or nightmares are just that. You really do not need anything. Of course, in a real emergency, the office there can arrange for anything but I did not see anyone needing it among hundreds who were my co-participants. One comes prepared also for these 11 days so it is not that one have suddenly vanished from the face of the Earth.

Communication in general is overhyped, among humans as well as among machines. Silence can be a powerful conveyor of many things as we reckon, but we are fast losing this instinct also in this excessively noisy world where shouting is the norm. Excessive communication is time and energy consuming, and peace eroding. We tend to lie, make excessive claims, bitch about someone, gossip, and all that when we over-communicate. Truth is straightforward and can be conveyed with very little effort in few words. We have always known that great people, sages, saints, true leaders, were men of few words. A key aspect of good communication is listening which is also being lost since everyone wants to talk and be heard. Many management and self-help books preach and teach how to be loud and clear. All these are signs of negative effects of (over) communication on sanity and wisdom.

Obviously these 11 days cannot be extrapolated for entire life, but definitely one can cut down 80% of excess communication and eliminate 90-95% of media overload.

And with this perspective, we realize that the great communication technology is actually overkill and has perhaps many negative side-effects (and we are not even going to discuss social media). And it does not make a better team just by having better communication tools.

Technology is Artificial by Design

The fundamental postulate on which this chapter is based is that Nature is sinless and man becomes sinful when it gets away from Nature and lands into an artificial environment. Earlier we cited a story that explains how a man is influenced by the environment and behaves accordingly. Therefore, alignment with Nature is more likely to keep away from sins. We consider Nature sinless, because we do not see any evil design in the natural ecosystem. Even carnivores prey only for food and do not kill beyond their need. Nature is always providing without any prejudices and biases to every creature, man included. It is man who is going beyond need and driven by greed that leads to the transgression of Nature. Today, the way mankind is living, we will need 1.7 Earths to produce the required resources, and if lifestyle of the whole population is like the USA, then we will need 5 Earths! Greed and transgressions are the sinful traits in man-made environment and do not exist in Nature by design but are developed in the unnatural environment that we call artificial. The dictionary meaning of artificial is man-made as against made by Nature. Technology is surely artificial by this dictionary meaning. But we want to apply the word artificial much beyond dictionary meaning. Look at the thesaurus' meaning also.

When we say something is artificial, for example artificial jewelry, we mean many adjectives like synthetic, fake, imitation, mock, ersatz, faux, substitute, replica, reproduction; man-made, manufactured, fabricated, inorganic; informal pretend, phony etc. Or in another example when we say artificial smile, we mean many adjectives like insincere, feigned, false, unnatural, contrived, put-on, exaggerated, forced, labored, strained, hollow; informal pretend, phony, bogus etc. In nutshell artificial implies poor or substandard or definitely inferior. That is exactly what we want to point out about the character of technology that is going against Nature.

Since our focus in this book is Information Technology, we will compare and contrast its key ingredient that is Software with Nature to get some more perspective.

From Atoms & Molecules to Bits & Bytes

Fundamentally most things that we consume or use, come from Nature. The technology essentially transforms natural things to create things of use for mankind. Iron ore is transformed to steel, which is transformed to tools or buildings etc. Food-grains and fruits etc., are transformed to flour, pulp etc., and packaged to be transported across the world using trains, planes, ships etc. Crude oil is transformed into Petrol, Diesel and plethora of polymers and plastics, which is core to modern life-style. Sand or silica is transformed into Chips that make all computing devices including mobile phones. A few decades back, GE was able to produce artificial diamonds by creating similar pressures and temperatures that exist at depths of the Earth and compressed carbon particles into diamonds. It was a breakthrough that compressed a million-year process into a few hours in a sophisticated lab. But still the carbon atoms used in this are from Nature. So practically everything is from Nature.

Carl Sagan once profoundly quoted "if you wish to make an apple pie from scratch, you must invent the universe". Even if we create something in the lab, say a new compound or chemical, basically everything comes from Nature. We might create (isolate) some fundamental particles in a sophisticated lab like Cern, but imagine creating an entire universe. All atoms and everything really belong to Nature. But can we say the same thing for Bits and Bytes? Can we say that all our thoughts and imaginations also come from Nature? Or can we say a mathematical expression like a set of equations to *model* weather come from Nature, although weather itself is a natural phenomenon. The same mathematical model then can be represented in software, which is basically a stream of Bits, so do Bits belong to Nature? Perhaps not.

An important invention of the 20th century was movement from Analog to Digital, which fundamentally meant that you could convert an Analog signal, say voice, to its digital representation as a stream of bits. The Digital signal can be stored, processed, transmitted, retrieved, played-back etc., at relative ease since bits can be stored as 0 and 1 and can be transmitted in *packets*. This is fundamental of all technologies like telecommunication, internet, audio, video, etc. Barring electricity, almost all signals that you deal with these days are digital. So, that was true digital known to most engineers before the word *Digital* was hijacked by research analysis and consulting companies recently and now it means something different and confusing. We have already discussed how the IT industry manufactures buzzwords and sometimes recycles some buzzwords. We have also covered the game plan of research analyst companies in the chapter Technology Innovations.

Bits can represent any mathematics (logic or equation etc.), and any signal. Bits representing a logic called Program can be executed (or run) on a computer, while bits representing signals can be stored, processed and transmitted. The Internet is fundamentally the biggest medium of transmission of these packets of bits across the world. Culmination of telecommunication and computing technologies is thus based on these bits at the core.

Software is completely man-made with no natural ingredient and no natural equivalent. The Laws of gravity or Newton's equations of force and momentum etc. are not applicable to it. Although the computer or mobile phone it runs on, is fundamentally made from things from Nature but its main technology inside or the *Life* is software – which is man created. So, mainstream computing and communication technology is dealing with bits, which have no *connect* with Nature.

Relatively speaking, the technologies until the Industrial revolution were nearer to Nature, because they were largely using raw materials from Nature, and the technologies in the Information Age are based on bits and software which are fundamentally disconnected from Nature, hence un-natural or artificial by design.

Table below compares Nature with Software Technology with some amazing equivalences and stark contrasts.

Nature	Software Technology
Atoms & Molecules, Cells	Bits & Bytes
Physical world	Virtual world
Life is the main entity or magic	Application or App is the main entity or magic
Life itself is doer and enjoyer	Application is doer but Man is the beneficiary
Life has a beginning and an end	Applications have beginning but no definite end
Life needs oxygen, water, calories (food)	Applications only needs calories (electricity) to run
Governed by Laws of Nature like Gravity & Force, limitation of speed of light apply	Only speed of light limitation is applicable on Bits and Bytes
Evolutionary – Growth is a continuous function with limits imposed by Nature	Revolutionary – Growth has no real limitations
Completely Evolved on its own or Created (by whom) is an eternal quest for Man	Created by Man for sure
Purpose for Life and Nature is another eternal quest	Purpose of Application and Software world is to serve Man and Business

The crux of Nature is Life and the crux of Software is Application. Like life-forms, an Application can accomplish tasks, take decisions, follow instructions, etc. There are so many similarities between life and Application that we say it is *up and running*, it is down, it is under maintenance, it is old, etc. We even talk about health of Application – a healthy application does not require maintenance and is error free, while an unhealthy or old application needs constant repairs and has lower reliability with fixes that have been done on it over a period of time by different people (software engineers). Applications *age* and with age they require more attention and efforts to ensure them running. Corporates that majorly run on IT, take a periodic look at their set of applications (called application *portfolio*) to assess overall health of their collective applications.

Applications are treated so similar to real life-forms, yet they are not life-forms. They cannot self-heal, procreate and self-adopt to a changing environment. They cannot think and feel like we do. Although some form of software known as *viruses* can be so designed as to replicate across a network mimicking a virus. A real tiny virus can bring down the whole world as we are witnessing in this Covid-19 pandemic.

The ultimate software Application is perhaps the brain of a general-purpose Robot, which can completely mimic human behavior in nearly all walks of life. Of course, such a Robot does not exist yet but more than 40 years ago Isaac Asimov in his science fiction weaved fantastic stories about our lives in the presence of such general-purpose Robots. They are perfect order takers, perfect factory-workers, perfect butlers, perfect babysitters, perfect space travelers, and many such things. Going further, one can think of replicating himself or herself in a *specially purposed robot* which in a way extends one's own life into an infinite future. That Robot will look like you (if you decide), will behave like you, will make decisions like you, etc. And they are postulating that one needs not write this complex program, instead the technology of AI and Deep Learning will *generate* this program by observing you for days and weeks and then bingo – here you are in your own true *Avatar*! And that is a perfect example of Artificial Life - life-like capabilities in a life-less machine.

Machines were key to the Industrial revolution and since then we are actually machine dependent in all walks of life. All our daily use devices and gadgets like, car, lift, airplane, mobile phone, laptop, mixer-grinder, air-conditioner, etc., are all machines. Factories essentially run on machines like lathes, cranes, Robotic arms, CNC machines, etc. And now we have something called Digital Twin which is a software model of a physical machine except that it has no real moving parts so it can not do real work like machines do. But it can simulate the machine behavior in software and can reveal important characteristics of real machines in real-world conditions, which helps in understanding and analyzing the performance of real machines. Aircraft engines, turbines, and such expensive machines whose downtime means loss of business, are better serviced and maintained using Digital Twins. One can run a Digital Twin of an Aircraft engine without burning precious fuel and without subjecting the real engine to the wear-and-tear, which reduces its life. Many engine parameters can be monitored in this manner, which helps reduce the downtime by scheduling proper maintenance. So, using software one can build artificial machines also. Many business models are being invented around Digital Twins as one can imagine.

Although we have not discussed Money, but most money resides in the form of bits-and-bytes inside banks and stock exchanges and is transacted through software Applications over the Internet. We have artificial man or *Avatar*, artificial machine or *Digital Twin,* and artificial or *Virtual* money - all courtesy software.

From Barter system to Bitcoin

In every role of life, we all are providing service to someone else – be it employer, customer, family, society or country. Humanity primarily exists to provide service to humanity – so entire humanity can be considered as a giant machine-like service-exchange whose input is work or service and output is wealth. Real work generates real wealth. Money is the most vital lubricant to make this service-exchange run smoothly. Money also makes the world *enterprising, interesting* and worth *investing*. Originally money was a replacement of the Barter system and facilitated easy exchange of goods or services, but now money has acquired a central role in all walks of life and making money has become a major objective of life for most. It is perfectly fine so long as it is linked with real-work, and some luck maybe.

All fundamental goods that we consume or deal with, directly or indirectly comes from Nature. So, Goods and Services provide 100% real value and hence generate real money which can be used to purchase equivalent goods and services as per one's needs in this giant wealth-creating service-exchange.

There are many Industries that deal primarily with money. Banks, Credit card businesses, stock markets, currency-exchanges and Insurance companies to some extent, mainly use money as raw material as well as finished goods. Time value of money led to the concept of interest, which is the basis of the banking system and is a good *additive* to the lubricant (money). An additive enhances the efficacy of lubricant so serves as a good analogy here. Sharing ownership of business with the public at large is to share wealth and the wealth creation process is the basis of Stock markets, and that is another good additive to the lubricant. And covering risks of all kinds like, life and non-life, in exchange of money, is the basis of Insurance business, which unfortunately translates into selling fear in many cases, but is also a desirable additive. All these can be clubbed under Financial institutions and their major role is to lubricate the giant service-exchange machine by pumping the right amount of lubricant to millions of cogs-and-wheels of the machine. A business can be considered to be a cog in that machine which is meshed with other cogs and the entire machine moves through these intermeshed cogs. And with modern Digital technologies, money in the form of bits-and-bytes can be easily sprinkled far-and-wide inside this machine through the Internet. Businesses have become global largely due to this digital enablement.

But many centralised financial institutions have become very large and powerful and often found indulged in scandals and swindling. It is like lubricants are holding the whole machine to a ransom. Here comes Bitcoin based on Blockchain technology, a panacea for all ills of banking. Blockchain is a mechanism and algorithm that makes ownership and transfer of money without a central agency like a bank. The algorithm based on factoring of very large-prime numbers is far more trustworthy and reliable than centralized banks. Unfortunately, it consumes a huge amount of computing effort for every transaction hence it is yet to be seriously implemented at large-scale, and there may be vested interests against it as well. Blockchain has the potential to seriously disrupt or replace any centralized system including banking, insurance, stock-exchanges, and even governments.

Illusion of Value Add – Evils of Virtual Money

Every meaningful human activity in any kind of business or enterprise adds some value to the world at large and money is the best representation of that value-add. But if the activity is not adding any value to the world but still generating money (legally) then that money is virtual. Wealth is the sum total of real and virtual money since virtual money is also money with the same buying power as real money. Unfortunately, it is like saying whether back or while – money is money. The rise of virtual money and its increasing proportion in the overall wealth is a leading cause of economic frauds -- this is depicted in figure 3.

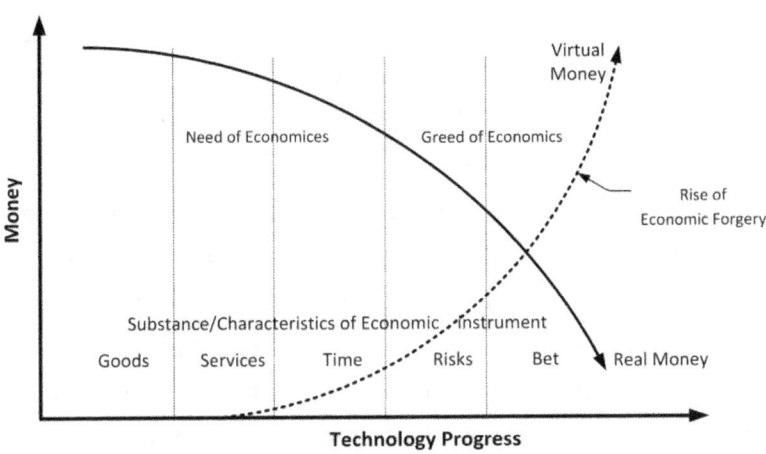

Figure 3: Virtual Money- Illusion of value add

Stock markets have emerged as money-making machines (almost like slot-machines) where money is increasingly delinked from real goods and services. Apart from being a lubricant in the giant service-exchange machine, they have become giant money-making machines themselves. One fellow buys and the other fellow sells and after sometime the sequence reverses. The company whose stocks are being bought and sold is doing the same business with the same profitability and same business model, etc. Without going into the nitty-gritties, it is obvious that a lot of money changes hands based on speculations or betting. And actually, no money is changing hands also as it is still lying in the same banks in different accounts before and after the transactions. Many speculation-based business models have sprung-up to keep millions of people busy doing virtual work of "money generating money" instead of meaningful work generating money. Future and Options, Hedge funds, Derivatives of all kinds, etc., are new-age business models where billions of dollars' worth of transactions take place every day.

The economic crash of 2008 resulting from packaging home-loans and creating securities out of such debt was a clear example of evils of virtual money. In more technical terms it is expressed as *"Securitization allowed for shifting of risk and lax underwriting standards: Many mortgages were bundled together and formed into new financial instruments called mortgage-backed securities, in a process known as securitization. These bundles could be sold as (ostensibly) low-risk securities partly because they were often backed by credit default swaps insurance. Because mortgage lenders could pass these mortgages (and the associated risks) on in this way, they could and did adopt loose underwriting criteria (due in part to outdated and lax regulation)."*

A common person can easily understand any situation dealing with real money. But here it is all virtual money and terms like Securitization are crafty ways to impress a commoner but it is plain fraud. The overall domino-like sequence of events leading to collapse of major financial institutions like Lehman Brothers, is still being understood in its entirety, but fundamentally it is the rise of virtual money linked with the rise of unreason that we have seen earlier. What else could explain almost back-to-back mega-frauds within just 7 years – the Dot.com bust in 2001-02 and the subprime crisis in 2008. Surprisingly, or not so surprisingly, the stock-markets went into pits but bounced back pretty quickly after both these catastrophes to newer highs since it heavily relies on virtual money which has very high buoyancy.

Technology has provided supreme ease with which one can go about doing such transactions of on-line buying and selling of shares, leading to millions of people joining this *wealth creation frenzy*. Many get addicted to this buying-selling madness, eventually benefitting banks, stock markets and some middlemen who all make real money on a per-transaction or commission basis. It may not be necessarily bad as it generates huge employment and anyway there is not so much real-work left to do in the modern world which is increasingly becoming automation driven. But a large number of very intelligent, highly educated and talented people want to do this kind of virtual work which actually adds no value to the world at large. These intelligent folks are also responsible for dot.com and subprime crisis and subsequent economic melt-down. Virtual money can be generated with relative ease but it also evaporates pretty fast. But hard-earned money generated from real-work is also eroded in the process of melt-down.

A simple real work, like door-to-door selling of toilet-cleaners adds some real value for the buyer in terms of convenience, and for the manufacturer to sell some additional units. This value-addition is converted into money, part of which is paid to the sales-person. But in case of virtual-work what value-add is being done to any one or to any system but to the self? The day-trader takes some risk in speculating the market movements based on some data and some hunch, but there is no *service* being provided to anyone apart from self-employment and generally helping in some money circulation. World gains nothing and even the person doing it, mostly will not make anything in the long-run as it averages out. And this kind of money circulation is like very high current flowing in an electric circuit under very high voltage but it cannot light even a zero-watt bulb because the voltage and current are completely out of phase.

In our giant service-exchange machine, this kind of business is a cog or gear which is not meshed with any other cog, spinning on its own and consuming fuel and lubricant from the world at large. The fuel and lubricant actually come from the real work of some other people and hence this money making though betting actually reduces real worth of money.

People who take long-term bets on certain companies or sectors and who stay invested for a while and are serious shareholders, can be said to be doing some value-add in terms of infusing their capital and goodwill for possible business growth. But otherwise it is purely virtual, non-value-add work. We will touch on this aspect again in the chapter titled Technology is largely Self-serving.

While reflecting on the above, a childhood story can lighten the mood.

Two boys decided to make some money by selling peanuts in a *Mela* (village exhibition) that was going on in a nearby village. They purchased a bagful of peanuts each and started walking towards the other village which was a little far. After some walking, one boy felt hungry. He had peanuts for sale that he thought he should not consume himself. Incidentally he was still left with one rupee after his peanut purchase so he decided to buy peanuts from the other boy who was happy to make his first sale. After some more walking, the other boy also felt hungry but it was against his business ethics also to eat what was meant to be sold. So, he also buys peanuts from the first boy from the same one rupee which came to his possession just a short while ago. After some more walk, the first boy felt hungry again so he buys peanuts from the other boy again. And this process continues until they reach the *Mela* only to realize that they have hardly any peanuts left to sell and one rupee of combined wealth.

Artificial can substitute Natural for limited purpose

Artificial things do have need and purpose. Like artificial jewelry and artificial smile has its purpose and need, same way even though they are artificial, technology has purpose and need in human life. Acceptance of inferior things has been successfully achieved in several fundamental aspects of life and technology in the food industry is among the most prominent examples. Application of technology in food is now pervasive at all levels right from growing it artificially, cooking in home or cooking in restaurant, or cooking and packaging food in factories at massive scale. Technology has introduced many unnatural elements in the food that has created health problems. One uses technology to buy sickness and then use technology to buy cure. Sadly, the cure is also elusive because the cure delivered by technology may not meet the purpose either.

Another example is the application of technology in the music and films industry to produce music and film. Now it matters more how much is your skill in using the features and function of music composing application rather than the skill of actual musical instrument. Analog is natural because the entire universe is analog and digital is artificial. I am sure that everyone will be able to understand the difference between the quality of a real piano and a keyboard. In films also the use of technology has brought the special effects in forefront and emotions and expressions have gone in the background. Emotions and expressions are the natural elements of human indulgence and they are going in the background.

Technology is like a hammer and everything - legal or illegal, moral or immoral, ethical or unethical - all look the same *nail* to it. So, a crook and a fraudster can use AI and ML to their advantage in finding right *targets* whom they can fool. Same technology is used by Police to find out potential rogue elements in a society, by income-tax department to find tax offenders etc. But somehow the crooked brain is ahead in any game and they have the upper hand and others have to catch-up. And sometimes, they might be two sides of the same coin - like the Computer Virus industry where it is believed that viruses are unleashed by the same companies who make and sell anti-virus software.

Is Man disconnected from Nature?

Man has created artificial technology leading to synthetic life so how natural man himself is? May be man is not part of Nature that encompasses all plants, animals and natural cycles etc. Everything is so organized in Nature with such perfect timing. A bird knows when to start creating a nest and creates a perfect nest without any training or supervision by adults - and finishes it just in time to lay eggs there. Millions of such examples can be given about birds, plants, animals, fishes, bees, butterflies, and almost everything in Nature. But not a single good example can be given about humans. Of course, we have genetic qualities that are inherited and some traits from earlier generations, but we come prepared for nothing into this world. No skills to survive on our own, no skill to cook or eat, no skill to build any dwelling, etc. So, somehow humans are disconnected with Nature from the very start of life as they learn everything from humans (and books and the internet, which are all man-made). We are not sure whether it was like that a million year back and whether we got dis-associated with Nature over a period of time, OR, we actually came from a different planet - metaphorically at least. We are on top of the food chain not because of any Nature given abilities but due to our technology and brain (or thinking capability due to a large brain). Since we may not be part of Nature, we do not care about Nature and so indulge in destroying it without any sixth-sense that would have warned us not to do it. Someone cutting a jungle would have otherwise received an inbuilt message (intuition) not to do so. No other animal takes more than what it needs at any given point from Nature, but we humans hoard and plan for an infinite future. Ants, bees, squirrels and some others do stash excess food but that is mainly to factor-in scarcity in impending season like winter. Squirrels are also forgetful and many of their stashed seeds are not dug-up and eaten by them and thus end-up becoming trees. We happily plunder and commercialize honey which bees collect with their unseizing hard-work. Nature has plans for all animals and entire flora and fauna, but (whether) we may have excluded ourselves from that plan by overly depending upon our superior brain and resulting technology prowess.

All said, humans are basically animals so do share some Nature provided instincts. Like a human mother will care and even give her life to save her children, just like a cow, other animals or birds do.

There are some survival instincts also and fight or flight is another example perhaps. But they are still nothing in comparison to what instincts animals have in almost all spheres of their lives - from birth to death. Nature guides them constantly while we have only occasional glimpses. Not in the distant past, in December 2004, the world was hit by Tsunami, which devastated large parts of many countries, particularly in South-east Asia. Thousands of people died and many animals perished. Many animals fled to safer, higher places just couple of hours before the Tsunami. Humans were caught completely unaware sitting and surfing on beaches while animals, at least the non-pet types or in jungles closer to seaside, moved to higher places almost automatically. Cattles in India died simply because they were tied and confined to four walls. There are many other examples where animals are able to sense earthquake for which there is no technology to forecast. Now there are Tsunami warning systems which actually work on secondary data like rapid rising of sea levels at some place and based on which some predictions can be made. But this comes nowhere near Nature provided instincts that animals have and either we have lost it, or never had it. The voice of intuition or sixth sense is feeble and humans need to pay heed to it instead of drowning it in the noise of technology, develop a sense of acknowledging it rather than ignoring it.

Metaphorically again -- whatever sin Adam and Eve committed, God might have given them a punishment by driving them out of the Garden of Eden, and gave them a thinking brain and free-will to get disconnected from Nature. That's it. While Adam-and-eve and we as their offspring live within Nature, we have no clue as to what's going on. We do not exist synergistically with Nature. We fight with Nature to conquer it, to tame it, to plunder its resources, to drill deep holes for oil and use that to create Gigatons of CO_2 to cause global warming resulting in melting of glaciers, etc. But we simply don't care as we are not tuned-in to Nature. We are logical, thinking creatures, but even is that being lost?

Technology is Largely Self Serving

Technology is largely self-serving. The amount of technologies needed to accomplish a simple task is mind-boggling. And technology consumes energy - although it is not visible or noticeable to most. A simple Google search is said to consume enough calories that could boil a cup of coffee and the Internet emits more CO_2 than the entire airline industry. Next time when you have a video conference call with your team over the internet, don't think it is really free in terms of environmental cost. It could be very low compared to really flying, but thinking it is absolutely free leads us to take it for granted, overuse and abuse it. As clarified before, businesses exist and thrive on technology so business and technology are synonymous for our discussions in this book.

Technology is largely self-serving

We all know that in the last 50 years, computers have become million times more powerful and million times cheaper. Personal computers came around 1982 (courtesy IBM but Apple, Microsoft and even Commodore and Atari are to be credited) and by 1990 the Intel based standard architecture was in place and so was standard software that you need with a personal computer. It was Spread-sheet, word-processor and perhaps calendar mainly and with Internet and HTTP (hyper-text transfer protocol) in 1992-93, emails and web-sites became a rage and were the main driver of business around the world.

Fast forward to today. Nothing much has changed on the business front – business people still use spreadsheets and word-processors (Excel and Word from Microsoft are main ones), power-points, emails etc., in the same way and for the same purpose using the same small set of features that they used 25 years back. And surprisingly the ten-thousand-fold increase in speed has not resulted in any work getting done any faster. The on-board computer on Apollo-11 which carried man to the moon and brought them back in 1969, was much less powerful than an iPhone today. The Pioneer-10 space probe launched in 1972 is still actively exploring the Solar system and going beyond, had similar on-board computers.

One reason is we do not need it any faster is that it was already fast enough for humans for most business and personal purposes. So, neither new functionality was badly needed nor an order of magnitude improvement in performance was needed. But the overheads to manage the Computing resources which is done by the Operating System, itself has grown inordinately complex and it consumes most of the computer time itself. So, this is an example of technology serving itself – and not the end-users. As an example, the number of prime self-serving processes (the processes that run in the background as soon as the operating system is booted and is ready to take user command) in Window 95 were about 20 and in Windows-10 the count is over 100! In the early versions of the

Windows the limit of RAM address that an operating system can address was 16 MB (yes 16 Megabytes not Gigabytes). When a reporter in an interview asked Bill Gates, why he had thought of keeping this limit by design, the answer from Bill gates was that 16 MB is an awful lot of memory and why anyone would need more than that!! Not only in the operating system, but also in all system software and application software, the overheads for self-serving purposes are increasing faster than the increase in resource allocation to users.

It is as if software engineers who write Operating systems are enemies of advancements in hardware technology by "usurping" all gains in speed. Obviously, every Operating systems team cannot be painted with the same brush and there are some relatively very good ones, but the most commercially popular ones are in this category.

Way back in the 1980s, we were amazed to see Intel – the famous chipmaker – releasing a roadmap for their processors (chips that make CPU). Starting with 8086, every 4 years or so, they would come out with 80286, 80386, 80486, 80586. It was unbelievable how someone had a vision reaching out into the 21st century at that time. And Intel lived up to their promise albeit with occasional delays and sometimes faulty processors, but hats-off to them. And there were other noteworthy chipmakers also who had similar roadmaps. The beauty of their architecture was not that each next processor was 10 or 100 times faster than its predecessor, but it was fully backward compatible. This means that once you write some program using an instruction set of, say, 80286, it will work on all future generations like 80386, 80486, without any need to change. Obviously to take full advantage of the speed and power of the new processor, you may want to rewrite some parts of your program, but it was not necessary. But as we have seen, most of the business world needs spread-sheets, word-processing, emails, etc., and that kind of software (programs) running on an established Operating System, simply worked on computers based on new generation processors. But the companies who developed these software products were also eager to catch-up with next generation architecture so they also kept upgrading or rewriting their software. Whether it gave any real advantage to the end-user or not, is a question because already the speed and performance was sufficient for most office workers and home-users. But one cannot sit idle while competition is announcing their next-gen software product that "exploited" new architecture. So, all this got into vicious sales-and-marketing hype and everyone wanted the latest computer with the latest processor (CPU) with latest software products. Every three or four years, the entire stack of technology – hardware, system software like Operating System, and utility software – were told to be old, underperforming and threatened to be out of support soon. So, buying frenzy ensued and all technology vendors, be in chipmaker, be in software product makers, be it a support services provider, all were happy. Technology serving itself is best exemplified thus.

The above scenario also resulted in the birth of giant software companies that still rule the world. They have tens of thousands of software engineers who work on just one product line, say Word processor or Operating System. With such large teams, one has to also invent work – so apart from upgrading for the next generation processor (which incidentally is a small part now), they majorly work on new features in the product and some new ways to interoperate within the suite of products, and many more things. The software creation which was limited to a small team of programmers in yesteryears, is now done at massive "factories" of software developers. In factory approach, each worker works on a small piece of code or small functionality across versions.

With such large teams, it is the sales and marketing teams who have to bring food to the table. Unless they make the users and companies buy and upgrade to their latest product suite, the survival of these companies with such large teams is impossible. Massive events are held each year by these companies to "unveil" new versions of their products. Who-is-who of the industry is invited to attend and research analysts (discussed elsewhere in the book) are specially invited and to write about (the greatness of) the new version, etc. (this has been covered in rise of unreason in more detail)

These massive factories are of two kinds. One is what is already described above, and the other is to develop, support and maintain the custom built, domain specific software that industries run on. The second industry is even bigger than the first one, but shares many characteristics of the former.

Technology creates junk and then claim to boast that technology helps in dealing with junk

Big data is a recent buzzword that we all know to some extent. Hadoop is a nice technology (architecture) with the underlying Map-reduce algorithm to tackle Big data to derive meaningful results or trends. It is majorly used in predictive analytics, user behavior analytics, fraud detection etc. But with many technologies including emails, mobile-phones, digital cameras, sensors such as wearables, social media, etc., most of the data that they generate is Junk data. The spam folder in your email is obviously junk data, but even in a normal email folder there are estimated 50% emails that are useless and so belong to junk data. And most of the junk data is produced by machines (technology), and then we create special programs or macros to clean it up. After some time, the clean-up program itself becomes junk data because some rules have changed. Technology produced enough junk of bits and bytes and although it is very compact, we all have terabytes of junk data in our hard-disks. Imagine 7 billion people on the Earth each throwing just one hard-disk the size of a *puck* (ice-hockey disk) into a landfill. Technology has made it possible that every person can afford almost infinite storage or memory. A terabyte was unthinkable as well as unaffordable storage space just around the time when the Internet arrived. Now a kid will have more storage on his or her cell-phone. Obviously, technology cannot think and decide how and why such storage will be used at individual levels, but other technologies like Facebook, Instagrams, Youtube materialize just-in-time to usurp all the storage space. This is another example of a self-serving aspect of technology. Whether it is memory/storage space or CPU speed or network speed and bandwidth, all are consumed mainly by the technology itself in proportion to them getting cheaper. It seems pretty inflationary - similar to the salary raise getting offset by inflation leaving one with the same standard of living. So, the self-serving Nature of technology creates *technology inflation* or some sort.

Instead of reducing waste, technology creates more waste. We have already seen how technology is hastening the new product/model launch leading to throwing away the older product. Until a few years back, all mobile phones had different charger pins. Even the same company created different models of phones needing different chargers due to pin size. Every household would have thrown away dozens of such charges after some standardization was set around 10 years back. But even now there is no uniformity and some premium brands have their unique charger pins. Charging is such a primitive function that it should have been standardized almost with the launch of the first cell-phone. But it took good 20 years and by then probably hundreds of tons of chargers were left useless and ended in land-fills. Chargers for laptops, tablets, ear-phones, etc., have the same story.

Einstein once noted "Two things are infinite: the universe and human stupidity; and I'm not sure about the universe."

Solve one problem to create another

Weinberg in the book "Secrets of Consulting" gives out a very profound fact of consulting. When you solve a number one problem, you actually promote the number two problem to be the number one. And when you solve any problem, the solution always has side effects – desirable or undesirable. Like, when you take a powerful medicine to cure some disease, you can not escape from side-effects. And sometimes undesirable side-effects are so undesirable that you decide to live with the problem instead of side-effects.

Electric Vehicles are surely a good technology to curb air-pollution but producing batteries by mining and processing Lithium etc., is fairly pollution generating and earth-depleting activity. And battery disposal itself is a big headache – if not for the car owner then for the car maker. It may pollute underground water and may have other toxic effects. And then the electricity used for charging might be generated from Coal-based power-plant which is much more polluting than cars running on petrol. So, these are side-effects, mostly undesirables, or to be watched for. It is possible that you are using Solar energy to charge your car thus mitigating at least one side-effect. Someone may argue and decide in favor of old petrol car as there is no uncertainty about either getting fuels every 10 miles or so, neither is there a battery disposal problem.

A familiar example to IT folks is replacing old bespoke MIS with ERPs that integrated all information across business functions. Fundamentally ERPs did solve inventory management and man-machine scheduling problems in one sweep and really relieved line-managers by accurately giving all sorts of information that is required to run a business smoothly. But ERPs have standard business processes built using best-practices for all major functions for a typical industry. Adopting them means you have to change your own existing processes (and mindset) to a fair degree and learn new ways of doing things. This usually invites a good deal of resistance from line-managers and usually consultants propose a change-management to deal with this issue. And there is no guarantee that after implementation, everyone will use it to its best potential without a grudge. We might have to decide between having a poor MIS (Management Information System) but high-morale line-managers, or a great ERP with lower-morale.

Another consulting principle commonly preached is to replace uncertainty by risk because a known risk can be managed, which is another way of saying replace one problem with another one.

Complications due to compatibility issues

Like humans, machines and applications/packages need to talk to each other or provide hand-off to each other. Standards like Internet Protocol (IP) and HTTP, XML and Web-services, etc helped achieve many aspects of such communications. But there are many situations where a same product's new version is unable to understand the data processed by its earlier version. Compatibility of file-formats is still a major challenge in enterprise IT. One has to write special adapters to make two packaged applications to talk to each other. There is considerable effort and people deployment to tackle the compatibility issues.

Technology serves us greatly in most aspects of our lives and the intention here is not to negate those good aspects but to develop appreciation that there is a considerable element of self-servingness in technology (and business) which is often unnoticed. We have to pay for it, not just in terms of money but in terms of natural resources and environment. Subsequent chapters allude this aspect in some more depth.

What Technology Promotes?

When we say what technology promotes, we mean how businesses are using technology for what kind of business promotion. Technology promotes unworthy and artificial consumption of everything – food, news, entertainment, games, etc. - beyond dangerous levels. Technology is largely being used for instant gratification and to promote a culture of narcissism or self-adulation as evident from Facebook, Twitter and Instagram. Again, we are not blaming technology, but excessive or in-sincere use seems to reduce the scope of thinking.

Technology abets exploitation

Nature produced oil in millions of years and technology helped to consume in hundreds of years. Technology like shell-oil helps you drill out every ounce of oil from every nook-and-corner under the Earth. And invariably, the technology which primarily exists for the good of business, makes overall supply more than demand, and then it helps promote consumption at vigorous pace, as if there is no tomorrow. So, it sets a vicious cycle of over-production and excess-consumption, all in the name of progress and upgraded standard of living. And it makes things more and more affordable by lowering the cost with increased volumes. But no one computes the real cost that includes the cost of all-natural resources like air, water, soil, and cost of pollution emitted and finally cost of disposal. What we are paying in dollar terms is perhaps one hundredth of real cost, but natural resources are free to be exploited without worrying about consequences.

Similarly, how to get maximum milk out of cows in farms and then how to get maximum meat -- all that exploitation is enabled greatly by technology to serve business interests. It helps drill very deep for water given the water table is depleting fast. It helps keep the entire mall air conditioned by emitting enormous amounts of heat into the atmosphere. It helps get a maximum catch of fish or prawns in all fishing expeditions to the sea. It helps killing of giant whales in whaling expeditions without worrying about their rate of birth. Basically it abets you to become a mindless plunderer of Nature, at least so far that has been the case.

Per capita Consumption of food growing

People are eating beyond hunger. Technology is helping people to become obese. Innumerable food ordering Apps have made it possible to satisfy the smallest of hunger at oddest of times with choicest of culinary delights. Excess availability linked with crafty promotion of food items have made even your fridge obese. And there is a ploy to make it intelligent and smart to figure out if its low on milk or bread, and order it online on its own. Earlier we used to have a single door fridge of some 200-liter capacity for a small family and more or less we knew what was in it. Now a 600-

liter overflowing fridge is a common site. And our visits to grocery shopping are not reduced due to larger fridge, it has increased on the contrary. Many of us are growing older so our food consumption should have reduced but that's not the case. So, it is all going to our bellies and then we try to burn it furiously by walking on treadmills. Consume more – burn more, seems to be a mantra of this age. But the dice is loaded – you will eat more than what you can possibly burn.

And a treadmill is a good piece of technology for indoor exercise in certain weather conditions, but a treadmill itself burns more calories than the person riding on it. It is the treadmill which is moving the belt under your feet with your weight on it and you are simply lifting your legs without pushing forwards, at least at normal speeds. So, apart from getting some blood circulation going and knee movements etc., which does burn some calories, actual push is generated by the treadmill. But the treadmill display or the wearable device which counts steps etc., calculates the calorie burn as if one is walking on a plain ground. And many people walk on flat treadmill which is like actually going downhill. An upward incline of 4-6 degrees is required to simulate walking which most people are unaware of. Using technology in right manner also needs understanding of some basics.

The current work environment, career and competition etc., makes one work very hard. But that work is mostly sedentary.

Unfortunately, in sedentary work, one burns hardly any calories and move hardly any muscles except fingers and eyeballs, but one feel hungry often for a quick snack. With thousands of options of great quick snacks through vending machines or food ordering Apps, you have anytime availability of best food. Easy availability of any desirous item is always a problem as we succumb as often as we wish not to. And this is actually applicable to all kinds of desires and it is a fundamental weakness of being human. But instead of helping to overcome this weakness, technology abets and exploits it. The values have changed too. Foodie was a bad tag for someone who is overeating, but now it is a matter of pride and indicates their status, carefree mindset and zest for life.

Coming to the supply side, the production, transportation and storage technology associated with the food industry have undergone tremendous improvements. Most countries are overproducing and forced to subsidize (encourage) farmers to *under-produce*. Technology has made it possible for touchless and torcher-less (really??) culling of animals in meat plants. Once H.H. Dalai Lama was shown a completely automated and sealed meat plant where cows were taken in through a large conveyor belt and canned meat was coming out on another conveyor belt. "Can you reverse the process? feed these cans as input and get the cows as output?" he quipped. Good deal of research also goes into how to produce more and more milk using newer medicines and injections, how to get only one type of gender from chickens, etc. Some 6 million animals are butchered for meat per hour in the United States alone.

Over-production is complemented by aggressive marketing. Consumer is the King who is expected to buy all - consume all he can and throw the rest. Technology is really a superb tool in all kinds of marketing – be it digital or physical, which we cover next.

Over advertisement and generating artificial desire

Approach of modern advertisement is not to give information but to create desire. And sometimes it goes to ridiculous extent like in case of Insurance advertisements where they almost convince you of amazing benefits of death. And if one survives without insurance, it would be such an uncertain, unworthy life. Medicine companies also indulge in promoting their drugs in somewhat similar fashion and as a reader one almost feels like acquiring that ailment which this wonder drug claims to have a perfect cure for. Obviously, there will be enough fine-prints and disclaimers which no one bothers to read. But honestly, we have not figured out why they repeatedly advertise the same product and the same message a thousand times – through TV ads, through newspapers, and now through emails and social media. Don't they think the reader will get *repulsed* by seeing bombardment of the same Insurance ad over 10 times in a day? Some luxury goods advertisements almost challenge you to see if you can afford such a good life. In the name of creativity, the creative agencies care a hoot about sensitivities, as commercial success is everything for them.

Almost all advertisers know who is the real buyer in the family. It is rarely the breadwinner who is supposed to decide which car to buy or which type of house to stay. Kids used to be influencers for such things and it was welcome, but now they are the sole decision makers - thanks to social media and all that business.

And now you have advertisements in context of what you are doing or seeing. Based on the content of your email, which is supposed to be private but never mind, these large companies are able to push relevant product's advertisement in the side-bar of your email very craftily. Exploiting natural language processing technology, they figure out the meaning of a conversation in a mail-trail and suggest some product in the side-bar. Very cool at first, but soon it becomes irritating and sometimes scary. You have no privacy left now when it comes to advertising. Alexa or Siri could be eavesdropping on your all domestic conversations to know what you are buying next. The old-fashioned TV and newspaper advertisements were irritating and could be switched-off or ignored, but these email and social media ads are under your skin. And now all information about you, your family and relationships, your preferences, places you visited, food you ate, etc., are a solid and most important set of information that can be bought and sold. Facebook made fortunes selling this kind of information to wealthy businesses and governments, and were scrutinized recently. During that scrutiny, it became clear to the public at large that *you* are the product that social-media companies were trading. Initially we all fell for these *free* social media apps and over-enthusiastically shared all about ourselves. A competitive game was set-up wherein the number of *likes* you get or number of followers you have, became a pseudo-indicator of your popularity. And many of these social media and search companies were famous for never advertising for themselves – so were considered to be very different and *cool* than a normal *for-profit* company. Well, it took over 10 years for the public to realize that they themselves were the *products* on which these companies made fortunes.

Nuisance of Fake news made easy by technology

We are also witnessing the phenomenon of fake news as the media gets embedded in every second of daily life routines. It is becoming more difficult to find out the truthful news from the ocean of data. In other words, we do not have news anymore in the media but have data and most of it junk data and it is left to an individuals to figure out the truthful information from that. It has enormous implications on the democratic system. Modern democracy started in England in the 17th century and matured in the 18th and 19th centuries. By the 20th century, it was firmly established globally as the most popular form of government. All the democratic systems were designed on the principle of shared accountability/responsibility and power. There are three pillars of democracy, namely, executive, legislative and judiciary. None of them has absolute power, and checks and balances are built in the system to ensure that none of them gets absolute power. Every branch has some power and the responsibility/accountability associated with that. We are now seeing the emergence of a new tone of mainstream media (to compete with social media) and social media as the fourth pillar that has power but no sense of responsibility and accountability. This kind of scenario was not envisaged when the democratic systems were designed and matured because the progress of technology was not envisaged up to this time. We are inclined to believe that all democratic systems need a serious thought on this subject to design and implement a next generation democratic system that will account for all the pillars.

Multitasking- Artificial trait imposed on man by technology

Technology is delivering almost the same utility as it was a few decades back, and is becoming unduly complex. Again, take cars for instance. The basic utility is the same, which is reaching to a place, but the whole idea is while driving, instead of focusing on driving - which is great responsibility and great fun, you take phone-calls, text, check emails, tweet, *Like* some facebook posts, eat hamburger, drink coffee, etc. So, you invariably multi-task all those things that may not be of great importance while driving but since these are all features provided in the car, you have to use it because all others are using it. This "me too" approach makes you forget the real purpose of your car or your driving - and you are happy to forget it. In fact, if you are just driving your car and doing nothing else, you might feel bad being inferior to those who do such multi-tasking with ease and elan. Car makers and technology makers are happy to sell you more and more technology which has little to do with your driving or safety or natural pleasure associated with driving. You end-up as a slave of technology thinking that you are its master.

It is proven that we excel and enjoy any task when we pay undivided attention to it. Multi-tasking is not natural to humans, but over the last century or so, we have become somewhat multi-tasked and some degree of multitasking is good and desirable in some situations. Truly speaking, we, like computers, cannot truly multitask. We can only do task-switching by dividing our attention in fine time-slices and in that time-slice we just do one activity. Obviously, some activities are OK to combine. You can walk in the park and sing or listen to a song at the same time – no problem as there is no conflict. Walking is second Nature to you so you walk without any specific attention while singing requires some recall of lines of the song – so, basically no conflict. But if you drive and attend a phone call – can you effectively multi-task? There are studies which show severe degradation in reflexes – which are extremely important to apply brakes upon seeing someone suddenly entering on road, for instance, while you are talking to someone on the phone. Talking to someone in person who is in the passenger seat is almost OK and does not take your attention away but talking on phone does some crazy things about the attention and your reflexes. Maybe it is how we humans have evolved with other humans sitting next to us and after a few centuries we might become perfect multi-tasker with talking on cell-phones while driving. But right now, it is considered to be very dangerous, but who pays any heed to this well-known fact? We all drive and talk on cell phone and technology sellers (car, cell phone makers, talk-time providers, taxi-cab aggregators) are interested in ever increasing sales. Lawmakers make it illegal to talk on phone while driving but do they ever enforce this sincerely? Technology lobbies are quite powerful to ensure lawful warnings are at best ignored – like warning about cigarette smoking.

Artificially shrinking the life-cycle

Earlier we had mostly physical products – cars, TVs, Fridge, A/C, etc. They all were pure hardware and their makers improved them continuously and came out with new improved models every few years. You had a choice to upgrade or continue with whatever you have for its useful life. And coming out with a new model of say Car was not very trivial. Starting from customer surveys, to figuring out new trends and expectations from new generation, new emerging markets, etc., has to be considered before even planning to launch a new car model. But the fact was the more models you have, the more overall you will sell. So, in every product business, there is a tendency to create new models for everything and push those models by aggressive means and by persuading existing customers to get rid of their existing model. This has been happening since the so-called Consumer revolution which might have started with the growing up of baby-boomers perhaps. Getting the latest models was considered a status symbol.

And now software is embedded in almost everything, right from toaster, fridge, A/C, security, lightening, cars and whatever you have. Software needs to, and can be, upgraded very easily compared to hardware. New features, new compatibility or interface aspects, new connectivity with other devices, etc, can be endlessly modified with relative ease. So, without altering much of physical aspects, you come out with new product with enhanced software. So, the overall cycle of new product release has shrunk mainly due to software. In some large and expensive items like cars, sometimes a software upgrade can be done on your existing models, which is some relief.

We already know how quickly main tools like laptops and mobile phones become obsolete and out of support, or out of fashion. We are forced to upgrade every 2 or 3 years while they have another 3 to 4 years of life left. And new models in case of computers and mobile phones are not necessarily faster or smarter. It might even be less convenient to you for your work, but you are forced by the vendor or by the society to oblige to upgrade.

Before the digital cameras and digital storage of photographs became common, we had the classical cameras and film-development leading to printed photos. That technology lasted some 100 years until the beginning of this century. We, our parents and even grand-parents had physical albums of their marriage photographs. It was a real pleasure when a larger family meets for some occasion to take out those albums and spend some very high-quality time together - re-living the past through those photographs. Many stories were told and re-told around each photo. We really understood what nostalgia meant mainly through such sessions.

Nowadays, you have probably a thousand times more photos stored in your pen-drive and you can click a photo from your cell phone while walking or driving and post it on your Facebook or Instagram and some people might like it. You have a fleeting pleasure for a second may be while the album viewing gave you happiness for a long-time. But we mercilessly phased out that technology and threw the baby of happiness with the bathwater for our desire for instant gratification. Kodak, which was a pioneer in Photo-films with a long history of being a leader in the world, was wiped out within a couple of years. Their case study as to how they failed to understand the new expectations and continued with their photo-film technology led to their demise. They continued to believe that physical photos will be always required as it was very cultural. But in this case, the technology of digital cameras and cell phones, not only killed the photo-films but the whole culture of photography, the whole culture of viewing albums on a lazy afternoon, etc. So knowingly or unknowingly, technology shrinks life-cycle and sometimes kills very good traditions and cultures in that process.

False Notion of costs

Industrial revolution made mass-production possible at lowest cost with consistent quality. Standard of living of the entire world was lifted as most people could afford most things that were mass-produced. Lowering of the cost primarily happened due to 24X7 operations of machines, cheap labour and lower raw material cost due to efficient, global supply-chains and bargaining power. Information Technology like eCommerce made it possible for global supply chains serving global consumers leading to unprecedented volume growth and further cost reduction for all consumer goods.

The production cost accounts for only man, machine and material. But it does not account for any natural resource like water or air that the factory would consume. Also, it did not account for emission of pollutants in the environment. At present (in the year 2020), we are left with less than 300 Giga-tons of Carbon-dioxide which can be emitted before we will reach a point of no return. A typical medium sized family car creates around 24 tons of CO_2 during its active life covering about 100 thousand miles, while an electric car (EV) will produce around 18 tons over its life. For a battery EV, 46% of its total carbon footprint is generated at the factory, before it has travelled a single mile.

The distribution cost and after-sales service cost are other significant components to arrive at the final price which factors in profits and taxes. Nowadays with online ordering, one can order just one small item, say a book or candy-bar and it will be delivered to your doorstep. Can you imagine what kind of logistics efforts and costs are involved? Obviously, it is all factored in the final price you pay, but compare it environmentally with you driving to a mall and buying all your needs for a week and carrying a trunk-load back. With all the route-optimization and whatever, millions of one-or-two-item orders travel around the whole cities in distribution vans. And then each item is packaged nicely in bubble-wrap and card-board cover, etc. You just pick your little pen-drive you ordered and throw the rest of the package in the dust bin.

If one adds all the carbon emission in such home-deliveries and adds all the packaging that mostly lands-up in a land-fill, probably it will be realized that what price you paid was only a small part – the major part is environmental damage. The cost plus all the consequences of consuming air, water etc., and polluting in the process of production and then distribution should be the true-cost that we must think deeply about. Particularly in these affluent times, anyone can afford anything if only production cost is the basis of price. We should also include the cost of disposal of anything that we are throw-away due to a new purchase. It is like multiplying the true-cost by another factor of two, which will make the average true-cost to be almost ten times the price we pay. It is unfortunate that we did not find any solid research-report to compute the true-cost due to eCommerce, probably because big-businesses will not sponsor such research. We are depicting a good visual and further discussing this aspect of true-cost in the chapter titled Real value of Technology.

Wisdom

Where are we? Who are we? We find that we live on an insignificant planet of a humdrum star lost between two spiral arms in the outskirts of a galaxy which is a member of a sparse cluster of galaxies, tucked away in some forgotten corner of a universe in which there are far more galaxies than people.

Carl Sagan in Cosmos

For the past couple of decades, we have been witnessing data explosion. Every day mankind generate 2.5 quintillion bytes of data (refer https://www.domo.com/learn/data-never-sleeps-5?aid=ogsm072517_1&sf100871281=1) at our current pace, and this pace is accelerating with the growth of the Internet of Things (IoT). We now even have a term for it – "big data". And others have capitalized on this with software products to sift through the garbage. There are analytics tools for making any sense of this huge amount of data, effectively turning it into information. Turning that information into knowledge is a lot harder, as it depends on the individual. So how do we get to wisdom? If you apply artificial intelligence technology or machine learning capabilities on knowledge, would it be wisdom? Answer is not necessarily yes. It is just using technology to make sense of information and knowledge and act upon it, instead of a human. Yes, it can do it lot faster. So where does wisdom come in, as it depends on the intent and the purpose. Wisdom has a grander scope and a positive purpose. Data, information and knowledge is a "fact", enabled by technology. Wisdom is the "truth", which technology cannot help with.

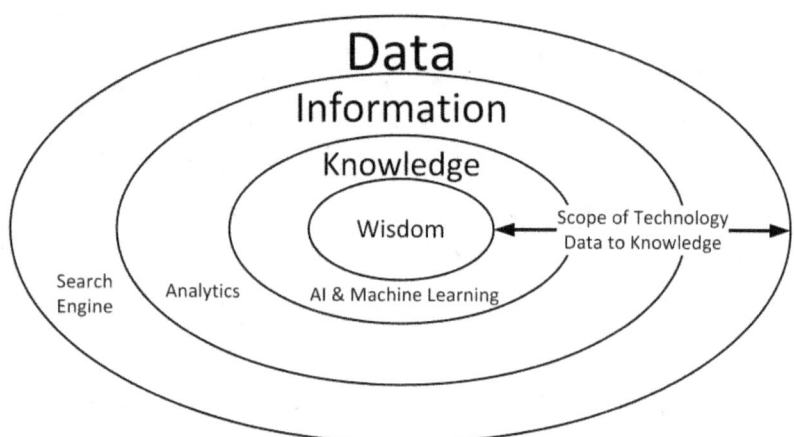

Figure 4: Technology Play in DIKW sphere

How technology is working on DIKW?

As we see in the diagram above, a little wisdom is surrounded by the vast amount of knowledge. Knowledge is surrounded by vast amount of information and information is surrounded by the vast amount of data. This resembles the model of our solar system. The 99.9 % of the mass of the solar system resides in the Sun but the size is less than tenth thousandth of the size of the solar system. Likewise, all the crux resides in the wisdom. Different kind of technologies work at different levels. For example, search engine technology works on vast amount of data and converts it into information. Analytics is the technology used to apply on information and derive knowledge. And finally, the latest trendy technology of AI and machine learning is applied to knowledge but wisdom is still not touched by the technology. Technology is not increasing the level of wisdom as depicted in the diagram below.

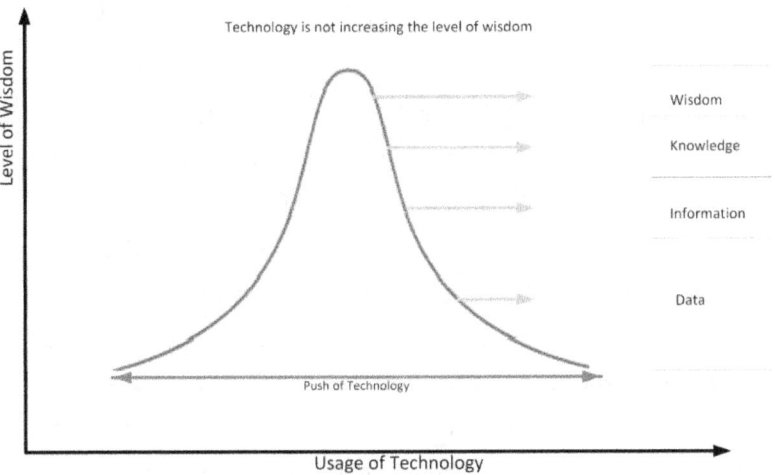

Figure 5: Force of Technology does not raise the level of wisdom

Now let's delve deeper into wisdom by understanding a bit about a very old concept called *Dharm* (or Dharma).

Every human being in civilized society has several roles to play in personal and professional life, like that of a father, mother, daughter, son, teacher, soldier, doctor, employee, employer, etc. *Dharm* is associated with each role which broadly defines duties and obligations in that role.

Apart from duty and obligations, some core values are also a very important part of *Dharm*. Living for those core values gives meaning and purpose to life. Such core values are often inherited from forefathers and cherished over time to become part of folklore, thus becoming part of a culture. And living one's life according to *Dharm* in a righteous way, itself becomes a very fulfilling purpose of life.

In human life, most of the conflicts are results of dilemmas or complications arising out of interenal conflict between various *Dharm* associated with a person. All our great epics, like *Ramayan* and *Mahabharat*, are based on such conflicts and pathway to their resolutions. Arjun in *Mahabharat* was in such a conflict that arose as most of his relatives and Guru were on the other side of the battlefield. Krishna reminded him of his main *Dharm* at that situation, which is of a *Kshatriya* (warrior) who has to fight for the right of his king. Krishna resolved the conflict for Arjun by systematically layering the priorities associated with each of his *Dharm,* and in the process explained many secrets and many aspects of life.

All great incarnations, great leaders, great saints, etc., have helped resolve many internal conflicts of the people around them at that time through their deeper knowledge and right interpretation of multiple *Dharm* and setting the right priorities in a given situation. We all call them *wise*, that is full of wisdom mainly for this reason.

So, one important characteristic of wisdom is ability to resolve a conflict arising out of multiple *Dharm* associated with a person in a given situation, and giving a *logic* behind this resolution so that others can also follow it or use it in their situation. No two situations and no two persons are exactly alike, so every person has to devise a somewhat unique solution to his or her dilemma taking help from scriptures or guidance provided by these wise-men. A person faces many such conflicts throughout life as his or her role keeps evolving and changing - from son to a father-and-son, husband, grand-father, from daughter to daughter-in-law to mother-in-law, etc. The person who is able to resolve all routine and non-routine conflicts with sufficient ease and who can also provide guidance to others in resolving their conflicts, is definitely considered wise.

This aspect of wisdom is very difficult to codify or convert into an algorithm (stepwise logic). There is judgment involved and several other considerations that go into coming out with a resolution. Try asking Alexa whether to upset your wife at the cost of pleasing your mother. Jokes apart, but most human decisions cannot be taken by machines, although machines can provide you with loads of information, can help you sift through massive amounts of data, can tell you previous cases, etc., but finally you have to use your logic, your judgment to arrive at a conclusion. IBM's Watson mastered and won the Jeopardy final against best human champions recently (2017) has demonstrated some remarkable debating capabilities and human-like logic, is a good case for discussion. It has also shown some remarkable capabilities in the field of Oncology (cancer treatment) by absorbing latest information from medical journals and suggesting appropriate line-of-treatment. Oncologists have admired these capabilities since they are very busy with to read all journal articles pertaining to new discoveries in cancer prognosis and treatment all over the world, so Watson becomes a really very useful *assistant* in this way. But the final decision about whether to try this new drug on a particular patient is still a human decision – and rightly so.

So, technology is a good tool in aiding your decision-making process but that's where it stops, and you should also stop expecting more than that.

Isaac Asimov, the famous science fiction writer is most famous for his work on stories around Robots. Specially he crafted many scenarios where humans and Robots interact in myriad of ways resulting into many unforeseen or unplanned situations where some tricky decision needs to be made. The basis of many of his stories were three laws of Robotics that govern behavior of Robots. So essentially, he proposed *Dharm* for Robots. Simply put, these laws prohibited Robots to harm any human being under any situation while protecting themselves (itself) from undue harm or destruction. Many conflicts and dilemmas arise in factories or outer space or at home involving use of Robots as the stories unfold into situation after situation. In some stories, human emotions are also involved like, a cute little girl falls in love with her caregiver Robot who was supposed to get dismantled having exhausted his (its) useful life. This makes the girl very sad and his father visits the dismantling factory along with her and they spot the Robot just in time as it was about to be dismantled. Here the Robots also show something similar to emotion and the reader is left wondering whether artificial life of a Robot can have feelings and emotions.

Now in the case of Robots, his *Dharm* or duty is encapsulated in an algorithm in three simple laws but different situations and different interactions with various human beings reveal that it is not easy to just follow the laws. Even here there is a role of wisdom and it feels like Robots are getting wiser with each interaction by resolving many conflicts. Wisdom builds with time. Many times, a human operator spots this conflict resulting in Robots going into an endless loop repeating the same task, and breaks the deadlock by his human intervention. So, an ordinary human being is shown to be wiser than Robots due to this ability to act as per situation and decide based on some factors, which cannot be programmed.

Finally, we close this chapter with the following key takeaways:
- Knowledge has no value without wisdom
- Knowledge is learned, wisdom is earned
- Knowledge has life span, wisdom is eternal
- Wisdom has grander scope and positive purpose is attached to it
- *Dharm* is integral part of wisdom and technology has little or no role in it

Wisdom and Knowledge

While wisdom is highest in the hierarchy of data, information, knowledge and wisdom, it still requires knowledge as the foundation. In the modern world the righteousness and wisdom are diluted from real meaning. Something is right or wrong is not judged on ethics but from the legal perspective. That means, if it is legal, it is right and if it is illegal, it is wrong. Legal justice works by this notion but not necessarily the moral justice and ethical behavior. A lot can be written about the justice system today. In US courts of law, a significant number of claims for compensation for torts are ludicrous, absurd, ridiculous, farcical, laughable, risible, unjustified, frivolous, or fraudulent, (I am deliberately adding all possible words to express my frustration) and we believe that the plaintiffs, who file such cases, should be criticized but in real life they win the award. All the persons in these matters are knowledgeable, but are they wise?

Clarifying interrelated terminology

The picture below is used to explain the interrelated terminologies in the map of *data to wisdom* process.

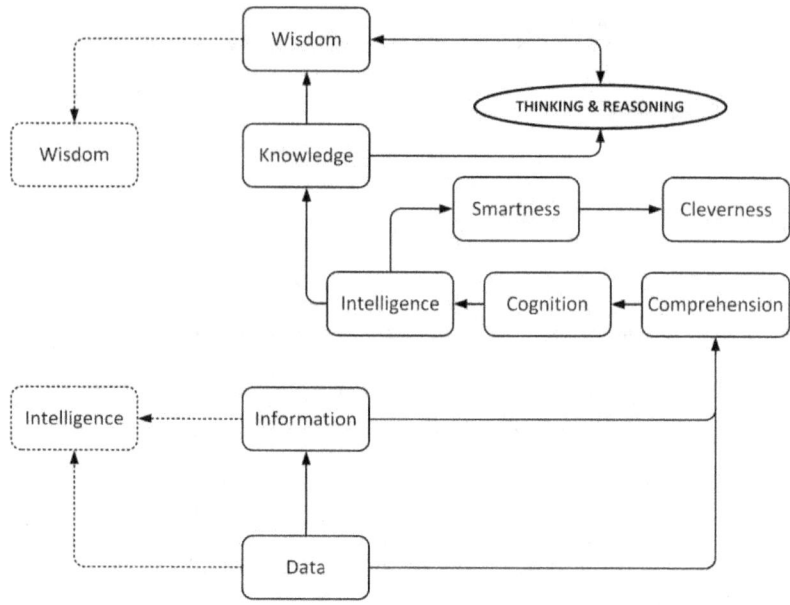

Figure 6: Data to Wisdom route

Lowest in the hierarchy is the data. Data is the absolute raw material that has no value without being processed and come to the next level of usable entity and that is the information. This processing can be in the form of organizing or structuring around some context. Databases in the IT were revolutionary tools to give structure to data to make it easy for processing and then deriving any information from it in the context of particular type of use. Relational databases were merely organizing it in tabular structure for specific use and then applying logic to extract information that could be meaningful. Today the technology is generating vast amount of data and that is actually a vast amount of garbage and largely a self-serving raw material. So, data is discrete, objective facts about an event. It can be quantitatively measured by cost, speed and capacity. The qualitative measures are timeliness, relevance and clarity

Information is facts provided or learned about something or someone about which the data is collected. Information is a message meant to change receiver's perception. It can be quantitatively measured by connectivity and transaction. The qualitative measures are informativeness and usefulness. Data and information, both are sometimes referred as intelligence also. Intelligence in one meaning is substitute of information or data for specific purpose, for example CIA collects intelligence data from all the countries in the world and use it to gain strategic advantage. The second meaning of intelligence is ability to acquire knowledge and/or ability to comprehend and understand the knowledge: This is the high value quality and acts on the way from data to wisdom and shown in the box above information. **Cognition, intelligence** (in its second meaning as we explained above) **and comprehension** are the capability traits that act on the information to produce knowledge.

1. Cognition is the process and/or methods to acquire the knowledge
2. Cognition is the process and intelligence is the ability
3. Cognition is about logic and algorithm and intelligence is the skilled use of reasons
4. Comprehension is the ability to understand the information before it becomes knowledge
5. Intelligence as explained above is ability to correctly interpret the information and convert it to the knowledge.

All three capabilities work in sequence in the path of data to wisdom to produce the knowledge., cleverness and smartness uses the outcome of these steps in the path of data to wisdom.

Knowledge is experience, values, context applied to a message. It can be quantitatively measured by contextual and evaluative attribute. The qualitative measures are intuitive and informative.

Smartness and cleverness are also the capability traits. These traits provide the capability to use information before it gets converted into the knowledge in the following manner.

1. Smartness- is the general-purpose intelligence that can be used before the production of knowledge
2. Cleverness- Ability to use intelligence before the production of knowledge.

While intelligence, cognition and comprehension work to produce knowledge, smartness and cleverness derive the knowledge on the fly and use it quickly in common situations.

Wisdom is collective application of knowledge that provides expertise and capability in the multiple tenets such as experience, grounded truth, judgments, values and beliefs.

Two meanings of Wisdom

1. Package of Experience, knowledge and good judgment for positive purpose and with true good "*neeyat*" (which closely translates to *Good Intentions*). In our book this definition is in the focus and above all the boxes in the diagram.
2. Knowledge of a society as a whole during a particular period of time: In the diagram it is shown in a dotted line box that is almost parallel to the knowledge.

In scriptures the two words knowledge and wisdom have been used interchangeably in many places. In ancient times, knowledge was deemed as wisdom because a knowledgeable person by default was wise as well. This is not true anymore. Today, a knowledgeable person may not be necessarily wise. Similarly, the wrong translations are so well absorbed in the public that it becomes a misconception. For example, the Religion is translated as *Dharm* in Hindi in many places though – The true meaning of *Dharm* is righteousness.

So, what is happening?

Knowledge is increasing but wisdom is getting eroded or degenerated. This is leading to several negative repercussions.

- We are drifting from the concept of wisdom and mixing it with knowledge. In scriptures knowledge was synonym with wisdom because a knowledgeable person happens to be wise by default but not true in modern times
- Lifespan is increasing but health is deteriorating; because we are not able to differentiate between health and age in the same way we do not differentiate between wisdom and knowledge.
- Availability of fresh and clean air, water, food declining even though we are making progress in in the level of prosperity because the measurement is not based on the natural value but based on the artificial value
- Because the knowledge is available to everyone but not the wisdom, we are not able to overcome, control and win over the evil ideologies

- Failure to prevent war and terrors despite enormous money on modern technological weapons

Wisdom of Nature

The wonder of Nature does not become smaller because one cannot measure it by the standards of human moral and human aims.

Albert Einstein

Nature and wisdom of Nature is infinite and manifested in its grand design. In Hindu scriptures *Panch Bhoot Mahatatwa* i.e. the five mega elements namely Jal (water) Vayu (Air), Agni (Fire) Bhoomi (The Earth) and Aakash (Space), form the basis of entire cosmic creation. Each of these individual elements is a grand design by itself and collectively they demonstrate the wisdom of design, build and run the entire cosmos including Nature. The ecology of Nature is extremely complex and we have all learned and witnessed it. Every component in Nature is compatible by design within a grand system. Just to appreciate an infinitesimal part of it, we have taken a few commonly observed entities of Nature based on our personal choice.

Trees

Trees are wonderful and adorable creations of Nature. We all know their role in producing oxygen and consuming CO_2 thereby giving us tremendous life support. Beautiful birds of all kinds survive and thrive on trees, and we get amazing Alfonso mangoes and many other fruits from trees.

Recent researches have thrown some more amazing aspects about trees. They are social creatures, just like humans, ants and bees. They live in societies, communicate with one another, care for young, elderly and sick trees, have a memory and learning capability, etc. Some trees, like Sal trees (in India) die of 'loneliness' when they are planted singly.

Perhaps many know Mimosa, a tropical herb that closes its feathery leaves when touched. In an experiment where individual drops of water fell on the plants' foliage at regular intervals, the anxious leaves closed immediately at first, but after a while, the little plant learned that there was no danger from the water droplets. After that the leaves remained opened despite the drops. Mimosas could remember and apply their lesson weeks later when subjected to similar situation. Memory and learning abilities demonstrated – QED.

It was discovered in 1990 by Suzanne Simard that there is an intricate underground network of mycelium or *mycorrhizae*, essentially symbiotic fungi that bind to the root of plants. The journal *Nature* cleverly dubbed it the *Wood Wide Web* and scientists have gone on to find all sorts of surprising ways in which it functions. It appears that forests are superorganisms with interconnections, much like ant colonies. On its own, a tree cannot establish a consistent local climate. It is at the mercy of wind and weather. But together many trees create an ecosystem that moderates extreme heat and cold, stores a great deal of water and generates a great deal of humidity. And in this protected environment, trees can live to be very old where sick individuals are nourished through nutrient exchange through mycorrhizae.

For communication trees emit a unique scent and are able to warn other trees of a danger lurking around. The fungal connection also transmits signals and trees exchange news about insects, drought and other dangers. Not only trees but also shrubs and grasses exchange information this way. Trees also use sound at 220Hz for certain messages like when they are drying up.

All this and many such amazing scientific discoveries are covered in details in the book "The hidden life of trees" by Peter Wohllerben. Any life-lover should read to really get blown-away by this humble gift of Nature called tree.

Clouds

It is well accepted that Water is the source of Life on planet Earth. So, we search for water on other planets and generally believe that finding water will take us closer to finding life there. Water is abundant, yet very unique, and has many distinguished physical and chemical properties without which Industrialization would not have happened. In solidified form (ice), it floats on itself - a truly unique phenomenon. If Ice did not float, the life of the Earth would not have existed or evolved, at least the way it is now !

But the more fundamental and 'primary' source of life is the Sun – obviously. And Cloud is the result of the Sun working on Water. Without the phenomenon of cloud creation and rain, water itself would have been pretty useless and would have been permanently stored only in oceans. No rivers, no snow peaked mountains, no lakes, no underground water – nothing would have been possible without rain coming from clouds. Cloud is a natural carrier and distributor of water around the Earth in a very systematic and rhythmic manner that rejuvenates Life. It wades its way through the sky where wind and pressure differences govern its path. Predicting its path and resulting rain is the hardest science where the largest supercomputers are always at work. Rivers complete the cycle by carrying the collected water back into the oceans. The river water 'recharges' or 'refreshes' oceans in some sense.

The above science of 'water cycle' is known to perhaps all primary school kids, but I mainly narrated it as preamble to "Cloud computing". Having revisited the significance of Cloud in the scheme of things for Life and Planet Earth, I certainly feel that the term Cloud computing is very apt. It takes computing resources lying in few large server farms (oceans), and distributes it, or makes it available in consumable form to the civilization. Computing resources are hardware, system software and application software of all sorts. We all consume these resources to do meaningful work and sometimes contribute new functionality hosted on some Cloud which is made available to others. Thus, the ocean gets 'refreshed' and 'enriched' by its consumption that happens mainly because of cloud. The Internet is the common carrier and distributor of these computing resources and also acts as 'collector' to replenish the ocean.

The very Nature of any Cloud - natural or computing, is Global. It cannot be a 'confined' phenomenon in a laboratory. We also hear some term called 'Private Cloud' which is some sort of contradiction. It is like boiling water in a tea-pot and believing you are making clouds that will rain in your own backyard. The technology of Private cloud is quite good and my friend/advisor calls it "Virtualization on Steroids". But I feel the "Cloud" prefix should be reserved for things of truly global scale.

A renowned Cloud Advisor and friend, tried explaining the genesis of the term "Cloud computing". Since the early days of the Internet, we always used to represent the Internet with a picture (sketch) of a cloud and various "systems" were shown connected to this cloud. That picture of the cloud became synonymous with the Internet and basically Cloud computing is Internet computing. But calling it Internet computing would have been so "technical", hence it is called Cloud computing.

Hats-off to whoever drew the first picture of the Internet as Cloud.

Nest

We are very fortunate that every year a little pair of sunbirds makes a nest on a low hanging branch of a money-plant kept in our balcony. The whole process of starting to build a nest to lay eggs, hatching and growing up of sunbird kids, and finally them taking off from the nest to the infinite sky, lasts for about six weeks. These 6 weeks are the most precious period of the year for us. We restrict our use of the only balcony we have and watch all their activities from behind the tinted glass windows offering a one-sided view to us without disturbing the birds. This year, it is the fourth year in a row we are witnessing this whole process and the nest just got completed yesterday for which two little sunbirds would have made some ten thousand trips to get small twigs, some special white dry leaves, some strands from spider-webs etc. We know in-and-out of nests since once the sunbirds kids hatch and fly away - they never come back and they never use the same nest for next season of hatching. Initially we used to keep the nest thinking they will come to reuse it instead of building afresh, but they are programmed to build a nest upon some signal from Nature and complete it just-in-time to lay eggs. But we keep old nests hanging on some branches so they can pluck some twigs etc, and initially we found they did not even do that. But over a period of time, we see them occasionally taking a thing or two from the older nests. The way they coordinate activities of nest making between the pair is very standard that we witness every year. Who does what is very clear and we believe one bird, must be the father, keeps a vigil while the mother bird goes about building and adjusting the nest and often yells at the father to urgently bring some other twig, we imagine.

Every nest is identical to all nests in shape, size, the location of hood-like opening, the padding for eggs, etc., to the smallest details. And all this is done by a pair of sunbirds, who have never seen (perhaps) another nest being built, and they have no training to do so. Where do they store the whole process and associated high-level and detailed designs? What do they communicate between them by constantly chirping during this building phase? Who tells them what's wrong at some stage? And many such questions we grapple every day while watching their fine work which happens strictly from sunrise to sunset.

And when the kids hatch, that is another process of rearing them by feeding specific diets that mother and father brings turn-by-turn. The kids keep making sweet noises throughout the day, sticking their open beak out of the hood in the nest for mother sunbird to put some food in that almost every 5 minutes or so. At Night, the mother bird sleeps with them in the same nest, so typically there are three live birds in the tiny space in the nest. After about a week, we are very nervous as the kids would fly away anytime now, and when they do, we cry a bit - happy and sad. They take a little jump from the nest to the nearby branch, try balancing and hanging for a few seconds while their parents watch from some distance and perhaps give some instructions or encouragement. Within a minute of some trial, the bird is out of our balcony perching on a nearby building corner some ten feet away and then off in the sky landing in a nearby tree or someplace. After a few minutes the second kid repeats the whole thing and we are left with the empty nest and wet eyes.

While Nature has gifted human mothers also with several instincts, but look at the scale and complexity of tasks that these little birds accomplish. And the kids - they just fly to open skies without ever getting some training and hand-holding, or shall we say wing-holding. What kind of programming Nature would have done, to get such a repeatable process? Is it all just evolution or there is someone working meticulously behind all this?

And this is just a tiny wonder of Nature where millions of such miracles happen every minute. All like a giant, flawless automated process programmed to the perfection.

Water

Look at the design of Nature in every minute detail. Let us start with the property of water. Why is the density of water the highest at 4 degree Celsius while the freezing point is zero degrees Celsius? Water differs from most liquids as its density reduces as it freezes.

In a lake or ocean, water at 4°C sinks to the bottom and ice forms on the surface, floating on the liquid water. This ice insulates the water below, preventing it from freezing solid. Without this protection, most aquatic organisms would perish during the winter. It has exceptionally high specific heat capacity (about 4.2 J/g/K), heat of fusion (about 333 J/g), heat of vaporization (2257 J/g), and thermal conductivity (between 0.561 and 0.679 W/m/K). These properties make water more effective at moderating The Earth's climate, by storing heat and transporting it between the oceans and the atmosphere. It has high surface tension and capillary forces. The capillary action refers to the tendency of water to move up a narrow tube against the force of gravity. This property is relied upon by all vascular plants, such as trees. All known forms of life depend on water and it is fundamental to photosynthesis and respiration. Liquid water can be assumed to be incompressible for most purposes and is an excellent solvent for a wide variety of substances both mineral and organic.

Fifty years ago, the common perception was that water was an infinite resource. At the time, there were fewer than half the current number of people on the planet. People were not as wealthy as today, consumed fewer calories and ate less meat, so less water was needed to produce their food. Now the drinkable water is fast depleting every day. We heard not in the distant past, that future wars would be fought on water disputes. In India, we already have serious water disputes among various riparian states and we do have tense situation with our bordering country up north on river water sharing and control.

Quantum mechanics to the Universe: structure of atom to the structure of solar system

- The atomic nucleus is the small, dense region consisting of protons and neutrons at the center of an atom. An atom is composed of a positively-charged nucleus, with a cloud of negatively-charged electrons surrounding it, bound together by electrostatic force. Almost all of the mass of an atom is located in the nucleus, with a very small contribution from the electron cloud. Protons and neutrons are bound together to form a nucleus by the nuclear force.
- The diameter of the nucleus is in the range of 1.7566 fm (1.7566×10^{-15} m) for hydrogen (the diameter of a single proton) to about 11.7142 fm for the heaviest atom uranium. These dimensions are much smaller than the diameter of the atom itself (nucleus + electron cloud), by a factor of about 26,634 (uranium atomic radius is about 156 pm (156×10^{-12} m) to about 60,250 (hydrogen atomic radius is about 52.92 pm).

There is an uncanny resemblance of the atomic model with our solar system. The 99.9 % of the mass of the solar system resides in the Sun but the size is less than tenth thousands of the size of the solar system.

Self-healing design of the human body

We all know that our bodies can self-heal and self-defense. Doctors have understood and relied on this aspect and prescribe medicine and surgical measures for extreme cases and emergencies. Food is, and should be our first line of defense for most ailments that we encounter. Many medicines are derived from plants and herbs which are kind of food items in a broad sense.

Not just the human body, but almost all animals and even plants have self-healing property. Even mother Earth which is the only live-planet known so far, itself has amazing self-healing capability that we are witnessing during this Coronavirus lock-down. So self-healing is kind of inherited property from Nature and all living beings get it free.

But man being man, we cannot sit back and allow ourselves to heal, so most of us go for earliest medical intervention. As soon as first sign of some illness appears, we rush to a doctor and rush for medicines. This renders the body's self-healing and self-defense capabilities redundant to some extent, and over a period of time, it might not self-heal. So, one of the key *mantras* used even in consulting work, is never to tamper with a system that is capable of self-healing. The Secrets of Consulting book by Gerald Weinberg is one of the classics that reveals many such *mantras* of consulting. A passage from the book reads:

The reason that ninety percent of all illnesses cure itself lies in "the wisdom of the body". Although "wisdom" sounds mysterious, its merely a poetical summary of end result of thousands of generations of destructive testing, carried on in millions of individuals. Most of these tests were without the benefit of modern medicine, so any body design that didn't have the wisdom to cure itself was summarily removed from the population. Each of us, after all, is the direct descendant of innumerable unbroken lines of survivors.

Wisdom of Crowd

Before science and technology came into its modern form, it was an established and proven knowledge that not all the people in a society have the characteristics that are necessary to maintain the health of the society as a whole and a much larger majority of people in the society do not have those characteristics. And this is true not only for the human society but also true for the herds of the animals. This is why the breeding of the right characteristics has been an important factor in the progress and the growth of the society.

We also know that the intelligence of an average person in the society or the group is below the intelligence of the top intelligent persons. Therefore, it is logical to conclude that the power and governing control should be entrusted to a select few individuals to keep the society healthy and strong.

Experiments and research in the area of crowd-based knowledge management have suggested that under the ***right circumstances*** groups could be remarkably intelligent and often smarter than the smartest person in the lot. That means, when the imperfect judgments of individuals are aggregated in the **right way**, the collective result is often excellent. That is the rationale used to coin the resonating terminology "wisdom of crowd". The theory is that if you put together a big enough crowd and diverse group of people and ask them to make a decision affecting the matters of general interest, then the crowd's decision will, over the time in iterations, be intellectually superior to the isolated individual who may be the smartest individuals among the crowd. The theory is proven to be correct. Then what is the catch?

The key catch is hidden in the right circumstances and right ways. First of all, it is important to note that not all the problems can be solved with the wisdom of crowd. Any problem, that requires wider level of cognition, coordination and cooperation can be addressed by crowd in better way but even for this there are certain conditions. These conditions include diversity, independence and a particular kind of independence where the individual in the crowd is working absolutely independent of others opinion, knowledge and influence. The decision of the crowd is driven thru the disagreements and not on the consensus and the compromises of consensus.

Technology has sabotaged the wisdom of crowd.

Three key points that make the wisdom of crowd erratic, are:
1. Media speculation: Journalism, like the medical profession, is deemed to be a noble profession and it is expected that it will provide the unbiased and neutral reporting on anything and everything. However, instead of delivering facts reporters and

editors making guesses at what might have happened rather than reporting what did happen and in overwhelming coverage. This impedes the process of absolute individual contribution of a crowd member and defeats the ideal requirement of wisdom of crowd.

2. Momentum of events: In order to make the right contribution as an independent member of a diversified crowd, it is important that the completion of the event has happened and the situation will not alter. However, the 24X7 exposure to the events - even after the passage of event and dust is settled, media keeps it alive till new event is captured that has potential to deliver TRP. This defeats that prerequisite.

3. Subject area hype: Extravagant, intensive publicity or promotion that is often exaggerating is now a standard practice in the society across all business domains including media. Hype influences the thinking and leads to the promoter's point of view rather than the true individual's point of view.

Because of the modern-day technology, all the three fundamental circumstances for wisdom of crowd are compromised; therefore the wisdom of crowd has become erratic. In fact, in the modern world, except for the most trivial matters where the media is not meddling, all the matters will deliver erratic outcomes, if based on the wisdom of crowd.

Democracy and the wisdom of crowd

Technology is instrumental in blurring the difference between democracy and the mobocracy. The hyper active social media on every political and social matter is running on the most modern technology platform. The figure 7 is a self-explanatory depiction.

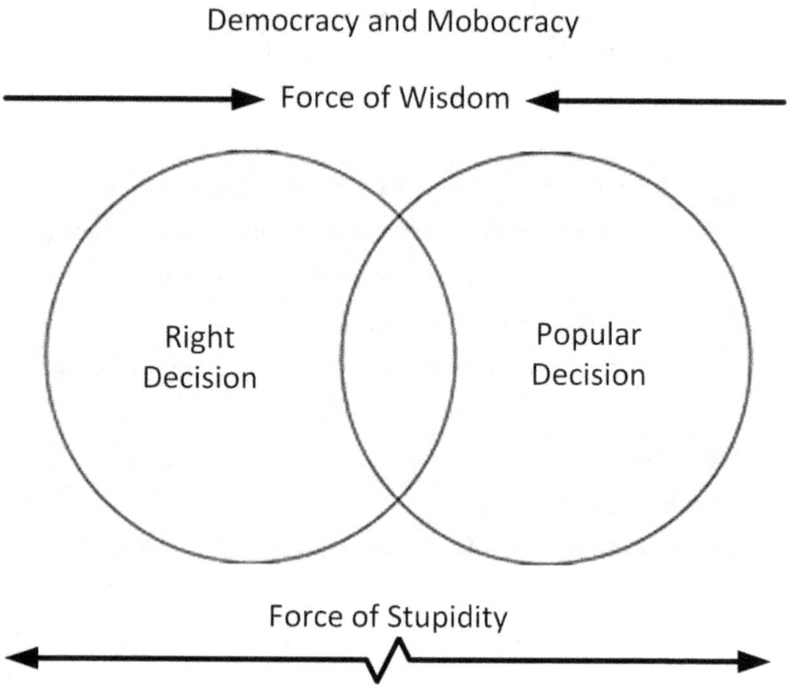

Democracy and Mobocracy

Force of Wisdom

Right Decision | Popular Decision

Force of Stupidity

Figure 7: Wisdom of crowd is not necessarily right

How the fairness suffers without wisdom is illustrated with the story here.

A bunch of kids decide to play on the railway track. There were two tracks, one is a used track and the other is unused. While all the kids started to play on used track, one wise kid figured out the risk and urged all to shift to unused track. All other kids would not heed to him. So, he alone starts to play in unused track and all the other kids continue to play in the used track. Suddenly the train arrives in its normal route and the maintainer has the right to change the tracks of the railway. When the train is about to come, from the far distance, the maintainer comes to know that these kids are playing on the track. It would be too late if he tries moving away all the kids from the used track. So, what should he do now? You might answer that he should divert the train into the unused track. For a normal mind, it is better to risk the life of one child than risk the life of many. But if you observe the kid, who is playing on unused track, is wise and righteous. In most common cases the majority wins. Just because a bunch of idiots make a group and form a majority, they can systematically enforce injustice on the whole society. Thus, the majority is not necessarily fair.

A recent ongoing example during lockdown where all housing societies are dealing with some issues related to safety and spread of the virus by outsiders. In our housing society, we disallowed entry of all outsiders beyond our main compound gate but sweeper was allowed to come and collect individual dust-bins kept just outside our apartment doors. So, he goes around in the elevator from floor to floor and takes out the trash-bag from the trash-can and puts it in his drum. Several members objected to this and proposed we all should go out to dump our trash-bags into the common drum kept near the main gate instead of this person coming close to all of us. There were intense arguments from both sides and the situation became very serious so we decided to vote on this. Over 70% voted in favor to continue with the current arrangement instead of going out and disposing our own trash. They did not think about the risk of someone who is exposed by many outside people and surroundings, coming up to our doorstep and touching many surfaces in the process of picking the trash. So democratically, we have decided to live with more risk and exposure.

It was very clear that about 15 families were very strongly in favor of stopping the sweeper coming inside and about a similar number of families were strongly opposing that. But the remaining 70 families essentially opted for status-quo which saves them trouble of going out early in the morning. Everyone has the same one vote, whether you are knowledgeable, involved, committed or not. In many other housing societies, they did not ask members on such issues and simply restricted all outsiders including sweeper. It appeared dictatorial hence we thought ours being a progressive society, going for a democratic approach would be rational. But democratic processes are no replacement for knowledge or wisdom, and are not superior to knowledge or wisdom in many cases.

Wisdom in Business

As our circle of knowledge expands, so does the circumference of darkness surrounding it.

Albert Einstein

Wisdom and Nature were in place before the mankind descended on the Earth. The concept of trade, commerce and business was developed with the development of civilization. The word business is derived from BUSY, that is keeping occupied in some activity. From that perspective mankind was busy without the purpose of commerce anyway. In modern civilized world, Businesses and Industries are real entities of the world for trade, commerce and making money that keeps mankind primarily engaged in work -- and work for the purpose of making money (and living). That is why most of us exist until we figure out some other purpose of life other than making money and living.

Every business has a set of business processes. The knowledge about the business is embedded in these business processes. For a retail business, sales, pricing, procurement, handling of return of sold goods, stock replenishment, recruitment and retirement, etc., are some of the key business processes. Each business process generates data for business and can be triggered by an event, like a customer placing an order triggering the order fulfilment process, or stock level coming down below a threshold level triggering the procurement process. Knowledge embedded in the business processes can be standard and common-sense or can be unique and differentiating. Like in above scenario, how and when you trigger a procurement process could be linked to threshold stock levels for sure, but one can also consider parameters like a long week-end or public holiday which will result into additional or reduced foot-falls, etc. All the situational knowledge cannot be embedded in the business processes and often a human, like a procurement head or sales head takes a call for exact order quantity. This kind of external knowledge or business sense is what companies pay their executives for, else perfect businesses processes would have been enough to run any business. In the ever-changing world, these executives also develop and implement new business processes. This is where knowledge is touching boundaries of wisdom to take non-routine decisions or taking a call on certain risks or opportunities based on external factors and environment. There is no fixed place to look for such insights and executives with heightened antennas pick-up any related or unrelated news or event and factor that into decision making. They use their own past experiences to deal with similar events or similar situations. They also make an intelligent guess as to what is likely move by competitors in the Industry. They also might factor-in how other businesses in other industries are reacting to such signals. Macro-economic factors, slow-down of economy, change of political situation, new import/export laws, and plethora of such factors are the part of awareness in making any high-level decision, like opening a new outlet or buying off a competitor. Business processes cannot capture all above. The best of technology vendors with the best of Artificial Intelligence or Machine Learning capabilities that they sell, still overly rely on the business acumen of their key executives for crucial decision making. That's why the pay of CEOs is in millions while a good worker gets only thousands. Business wisdom is about business acumen, business environmental awareness, insights, intelligence on competition, risk-taking abilities, insurgent mindset, etc. Obviously, this wisdom resides in the brains of key executives and board-members, who also leave, retire or get fired. So how does a company retain its wisdom which is its real asset? There is no short or straight answer but many of these aspects seep slowly into the culture of the company, so the new CEO or new board-member gets aligned soon.

Steve Jobs created and built Apple Inc. and his untimely departure from the world left a void. But the Apple Inc. continued on his vision, his quality standards, his aesthetic sense, the work-ethos, etc. and probably is as successful as it would have been with Steve heading it. There might have been more fundamental inventions perhaps with Steve at the helm. And one more thing. Many of the elements of wisdom about a company gets captured in its well-articulated strategy. Earlier the strategy of a company was supposed to be well-kept secret and now it is believed that articulating and sharing it with all employees and stakeholders and even sharing with market is good for the business. But the strategy document is still a piece of knowledge and real strategy is not a static document, it is dynamic action plan revolving around wisdom of the key leader. Leadership is business term for wisdom.

Using knowledge, as in business processes, one can run a business, but to win and grow business one needs wisdom (leadership). Knowledge is about what is there, how it is done, who will do what, etc. Wisdom is about what else is there, how else it can be done and who else is doing it. Knowledge is about how to sharply focus on your business. Wisdom is how to de-focus and see peripheral businesses and environment. Knowledge is about a business. Wisdom is about the eco-system surrounding the business. Knowledge is about content Wisdom is about Context.

Knowledge may become irrelevant with time unless updated but wisdom grows and evolves to become more relevant with experience. Context and Time are two key dimensions of wisdom. In the DIKW hierarchy, it is the context which separates wisdom from the rest. It is possible for Data to have no context – at lowest levels it is just stream of bits and bytes which can be interpreted in many ways. You can play a digital pattern of a document (text file) on a music player if you want to, although it will create non-sensical noise. Data with some context becomes information, like in a retail business context, the same stream of bits and bytes may be about recent purchase done by a customer. Business processes (in IT) and analytics software have business context embedded to interpret or understand this information and present results, enable or make decisions that are required to run the business. Wisdom is further up where context is much wider with the business at the center. Industry, Macro-economic environment, socio-political environment, environmental factors, cultural or locale aspects, etc., are some of the layers around the core of the business that provide context to it. With such wide context, some conflicts are sure to arise with its core purpose which is to generate profits for itself and its shareholders. What is good for profit may not be really good for the customers. What is good for cost reduction may not be good for the environment. What is good for today's shareholders may not be good for the longevity of the business. A leader has to straddle many such conflicts almost on a daily basis and this is where wisdom of the leader matters most. A leader has ultimate responsibilities or *Dharm* towards customers, employees and shareholders. Recently they have added society and environment as other two responsibilities to take care of triple-bottom-line. So, we do not just need knowledgeable business leaders who can make obscene amount of money for the business entity but we need wise business leaders who will run the business with wisdom who will make money without creating a hidden debt with society or Nature.

Any set of three points in space are coplanar meaning they can form a perfect plane regardless of their position in the space. But it requires calculated positioning to keep four or more points in the same plane. Nature with its own Wisdom were initial two points and then came Technology invented by man as third point. Almost from the beginning, man was an inquisitive wanderer and made some simple tools using his opposable thumb and tinkering brain. Use of wheel and igniting fire can be the formal birth of technology perhaps. Business, especially modern business driven primarily by technology entered much later and became the fourth point and kept itself aligned initially with the original plane. Now it is drifting from the plane and creating dangerous conflicts with Nature. Technology must be used in the business with wisdom to keep everything in the same plane that would be stable.

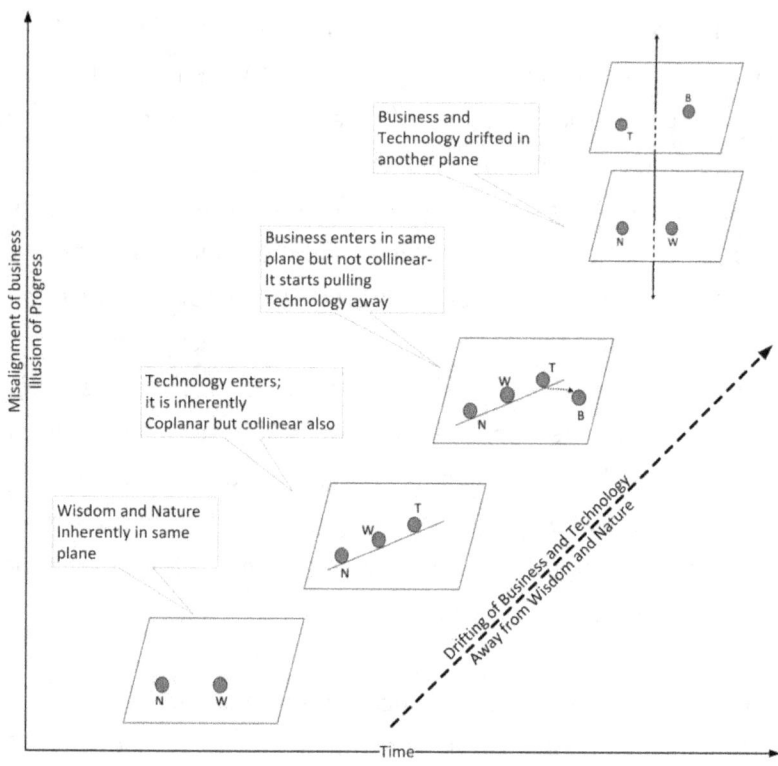

Figure 8: Business is the 4th point in the plane causing a rift with Nature

The illusion of progress, as depicted in the Y-axis above, is evident from increased greed resulting in exploitation of Nature, artificialness in life, and declining wisdom. Being on a different plane now, business is not concerned with Nature, and unfortunately technology got tagged along with it.

Real Value of Technology

Optimal Use of technology brings in real value. Recall during initial days, the inclusion of technology increased wisdom. Take Radio and Newspaper – the users became more aware about world events and thus knowledgeable and wiser to some extent. Similarly, cars made humans more mobile and car owners had a good degree of knowledge about working of cars, and science and technology under the hood. The case today is almost reversed. Is it due to the law of diminishing or reversing returns? Or humans are so designed that once mass adopted – a technology is taken for granted and no one cares how it works?

It is the rise of unreason that is causing the people to buy things that they do not need with the money they do not have. So, what should be the wise use of technology? Before we go to there, we want to provide some perplexing facts

1. The food consumption per capita is growing continuously as the food availability is increasing despite decreasing the physical activities in average person life and thus the need of calories per person is decreasing. Where is this extra calorie going? Towards

obesity in western society and that leads to health deterioration and thus justification in more money for technology in health.

2. Because of technology we are getting more and more versions of news and it is getting more and more difficult to arrive at the truth.

3. Need of information security is astronomically increasing and the security overheads are reducing the value yet increasing the risk.

We also want to refer to the book "Paradox Of Choices- Why More is Less" by Barry Schwartz a famous American psychologist and Professor of Social Theory and Social Action at Swarthmore College. In his book he broke the myth of conventional wisdom that choices available to consumers are helping them. He convincingly argued that when people have no choice, life is almost unbearable. But as the number of choices keeps growing, negative aspects of having a multitude of options begin to appear. Clinging tenaciously to all the choices available to us contributes to bad decisions, to anxiety, stress, and dissatisfaction—even to clinical depression.

Barry's points are

1. We would be better off if we embraced certain voluntary constraints on our freedom of choice instead of rebelling against them.
2. We would be better off seeking what was "good enough" instead of seeking the best (have you ever heard a parent say "I want only the 'good enough' for my kids"?)
3. We would be better off if we lowered our expectations about the results of decisions.

Use technology with wisdom

We want to echo exactly the same argument in the context of technology – that life is unbearable without technology but as the level of technology applied to life exceeds a certain threshold, the negative aspects start to emerge. We believe that we have crossed that threshold and witnessing the negative aspects which is overwhelming but we are ignoring those like fools. But we would be better off if we wisely use technology to the appropriate level in life.

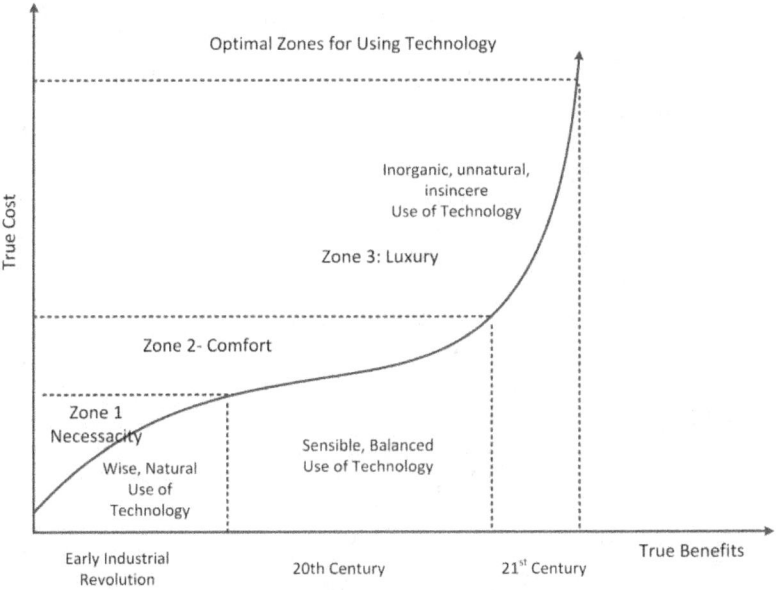

Figure 9: Optimal zones use of technology

We have discussed False notion of cost in the chapter What Technology Promotes. True Cost which is Y-axis here, basically incudes all the cost of natural resource, pollution, disposal etc., in the entire life-cycle of the product and could be as high at 10 times the price you pay.

Resonance Curve: Quality factor of technology

The quality factor or 'Q' of an inductor or tuned circuit is often used to give an indication of its performance in a resonator circuit. The Q or quality factor is a dimensionless number and it describes the damping in the circuit. It also provides an indication of the resonator's bandwidth relative to its center frequency.

Values for quality factor are often seen quoted and can be used in defining the performance of an inductor, a capacitor or tuned circuit. Similarly, the qualify factor of technology can be defined as the measurement of quality of life improvement with the induction of technology.

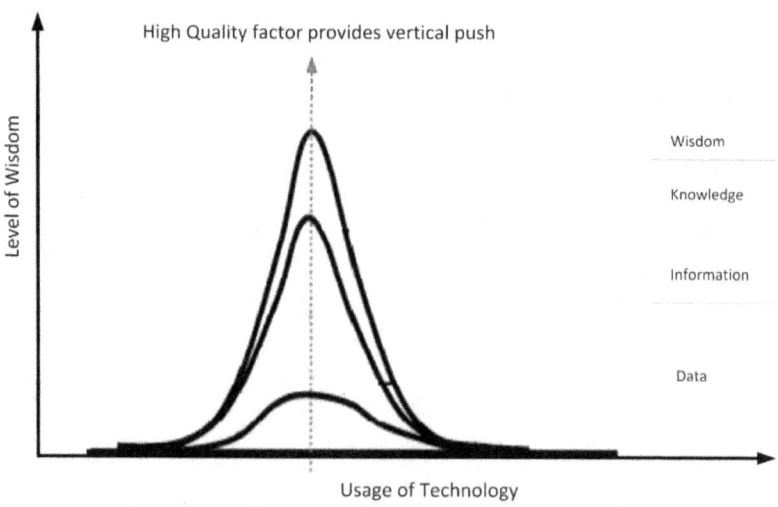

Figure 10: well-tuned technology can increase the level of wisdom

Tuning is originally and historically used for the process of adjusting a musical instrument to the correct or uniform pitch. Now it is used in many areas and most common use is in the process of adjusting an engine or balancing mechanical parts so that a vehicle runs smoothly and efficiently. During our childhood, a Radio-set was the biggest piece of technology at our home. These Radios were based on vacuum tube technology which pre-dates the current Transistor and IC based technologies. It used to have a small blue-green rectangular or circular display called Magic-Eye which played a crucial role in tuning a radio to right frequencies corresponding to various stations. If the Magic-eye is perfectly aligned, the tuning would be perfect and reception would be without any hum or disturbances. A fluctuating Magic-Eye would make a station fade in-and-out with associated hum and sometimes catching nearby station, etc.

It was a perfect example of audio-visual feedback in its simplest form – you see and hear a perfectly tuned station clearly. The tuning circuit or a radio consists of an Induction Coil, a Gang capacitor and a resistor. Out of these the Induction and resistor were of fixed value, and capacitance was increased or decreased linked to the rotation of the tuning knob. For a given frequency (of a station), there will be a perfect combination of Inductance and Capacitance which will make the circuit resonate on that frequency achieving a very high Q-factor.

Likewise, we think Technology, Wisdom and Nature are three main elements of the tuning circuit of the world, analogous to Capacitance, Induction and Resistance. These have to be perfectly matched to resonate such that we attain the highest quality of life and perfect focus while preserving Nature. If technology is way higher than wisdom, which seems to the case today, we will have an out-of-tune circuit.

A very good example of fine-tuning between Nature and technology is Solar power. Energy, especially electricity, has become the most fundamental need of humanity. Generating electricity by Coal, Gas, Oil is definitely environmentally damaging. Hydal power is the best way to generate electricity if it harnesses natural flow of water but artificial large dams have their adverse implications. Nuclear power is OK but dealing with radioactive disposal is tricky. So, Solar and Wind have emerged as frontrunners being most natural ways without altering or affecting the environment in any negative manner. Solar Technology has amazingly delivered a thousand fold increase in price and performance of Solar cells in the last 30-35 years. What was costing 100$ to generate 1 Watt of electricity from Solar, is now around 10 Cents. Solar cells have improved multifold in efficiency and life-time. Fortunately, most governments have *wisely* supported and promoted Solar energy and have committed to increasingly use Solar energy for electricity by raising its percentage share thereby reducing dependence on thermal power plants. Some respite in green-house-gas emission is visible due to the Solar revolution now. The Sun, which is the ultimate source of life -- is coming to our rescue again. In India solar energy bids for solar power plants are now offerings lower tariffs than coal-based power plants taking advantage of government subsidies. In Mumbai, we have installed 40KW Grid-tied Solar panels on our building roof which is enough to generate electricity for our six lifts, four water pumps and street lights. One key problem is storage of this energy for night-time use where batteries are default option. Many advances have happened in battery technology also and famously Elon Musk is delivering a total solution of Solar roofing in conjunction with power-walls (batteries) for households so you store energy in day-time for later consumption in the night. But if each car and each home need to have a large Lithium-ion battery, we will have other problems like disposal and chemical pollution associated with Lithium-ion supply-chain.

Many countries have gone for using the excess energy generated by Solar panels in day time to pump water up into a reservoir which when released can drive turbines to generate hydroelectricity which is most Nature friendly. Many governments are promoting this way of energy storage. This Potential Energy to Kinetic Energy conversion is best suited in our view. Science and Nature have many answers - we only need to tune-in our attention.

Lessons from History

The best starting statement of this chapter is "History tells us that we have not learned from history". This is a great fact that we have not learned from history! That is why this chapter is short because we have not much to write with pride on this.

Why have we not learned from history? Is it because every generation thinks they are smarter than the previous generation? Or every human being thinks he has to discover all truths about the world himself/herself - and so he/she starts from scratch? Or is it our overall/collective stupidity? Or, is it sheer shortsightedness of our very Nature that makes us see only a day ahead and see only a day behind? Again, like when Greta Thunberg says we have only time until 2030 and then the whole Nature will go into an irreversible change cycle through Greenhouse gases. But we think 2030 is very far. Within the same lifetime, we are not able to learn from our own past and do not bother about challenges we are very likely to face 10 years from now. So, learning from history has a remote chance.

If mankind had really learned meaningful lessons from the history of the past few hundred years only, then the world would have been peaceful and happier today. What is the use of learning other things if you do not learn from history and develop these two fundamental high value characters of the person, society and nation? If you look at the history, you will notice that the violence/terror and war are repetitively happening for the same reasons – the greed surrounding the power, money or lust. Application of technology has made wars even more lethal and intense. Technology has also opened up new battlegrounds that were not possible in the past and technology getting into evil hands is the biggest worry. This battleground is set for the war of ideology happening on 24X7 basis globally. Unfortunately, ideological war is also making the grounds for the real wars. Lessons learned from one war are forgotten within a generation and the coming generation is ready to go on the same path again.

In enterprise IT, we are witnessing a few fundamental mistakes that happen repetitively and to cite the most important is the tendency to solve non-technical problems with technology. Everyone knows that a fool with a tool is still a fool. Another aspect is that when the technology fails to solve the technical problem, they look at business to solve technical problems with legal tools. In the area of IT security management this is very common. As an example, we will talk about a Company that provides database service for multiple companies with a multi-tenant database platform. Due to the technological constraints, it could not implement the adequate security controls that will prevent the unauthorized data access. The solution for this was found with a legal clause in the service agreement that will mandate not to access the data of other tenants and breach of the legal clause was sure to drive the breaching customer out of the business. Thus, the legal fear was the tool for data security.

Epilogue

Earth provides enough to satisfy every man's needs, but not to satisfy every man's greed

M.K. Gandhi

This during the writing of this book COVID 19 pandemic was dominating the globe and we were in the state of lockdown. While we used the technology to communicate and collaborate, we came across the What's app message forwarded to us. This is a letter from COVID 19 to the human race. The original source is published here https://extinctionendshere.org. We would replicate the text of that video as the most relevant epilogue to the book.

Dear humankind,

Thank you, for being the super-host. I never imagined I would have the opportunity to jump to species as abundant as you. Most viruses only get to know only their original host animal. Many exist entirely in the humid understory of remote rainforest. We viruses are kept in check by healthy environments with diverse and abundant wildlife. But when you rip forests apart and capture billions of animals to feed your insatiable appetite for flesh and false cures, you bring viruses like me out of our natural quarantines. You introduce us to the new hosts like you- a super-host of eight billion individuals and counting - a walking, flying, swimming, human meat market. You make a third of all mammals on The Earth by weight. The animals you grow to feed yourselves outweigh all the wild mammals and birds on the planet. As you drive our natural wildlife hosts to extinction, you throw us life rafts bigger than the Titanic. Why would I not jump? As sinister as I may seem, it is not in my interests to wipe out my hosts. We all need other life to thrive. So if this sickness in your bodies opens up your eyes to the deeper sickness in our shared planet, it would be to our benefit. But my big question to you is this- "AM I ENOUGH?" If apocalyptic fires aren't enough, if vanishing glaciers aren't enough, if super hurricanes aren't enough, are the cold shadows I cast across the lives of you and your loved ones enough for you to finally confront the prospect of your own extinction? Only you, humankind, can choose to be the cure to the deeper sickness. Only you can choose to nurture the ancient oceans, forests and grasslands that nurture you. To bring back the chorus of birds and monkeys to silent rainforests, and to make **wise** choices everyday in what you consume and how you live. By protecting Nature, in all its wild and wonderful forms, you protect yourselves. As the Earth stops to take a collective deep breath, you have a rare opportunity to reimagine and redefine a new future. So tell me, what future do you choose?

By abusing technologies or by insane use of technologies, businesses have created a huge debt with Nature that entire mankind has to payback. Filing bankruptcy and getting away with debt is not an option. Nor there is a rescue package either. If the creditor comes with the force then what will happen? COVID 19 is the trailer of that.

If people are wise then they will make wise choices. Even though we argued that crowd couldn't make the wise decision, we hope that this time crowd will make the wise decision because the global crowd has witnessed the clear message in their own society. This time it would not be a temporary withdrawal from old habits. This time people will not forget this epidemic and go back to their usual spoilt ways to plunder the planet with the same recklessness. So we retain hope that all wise persons will collectively gather enough momentum to force wise decisions.

About the authors

Prafull Verma

Prafull Verma has a bachelor's degree in electronics and communication engineering and has over thirty years' experience in the area of electronic data processing and information technology. He started his career in India in the area of electronic data processing systems and later moved to the United States in 1997. During the past thirty years, he has worked on diversified areas in computer science and information technologies. Some of his key experience areas are the design and implementation of heterogeneous networks, midrange technical support management, end-user service management and design, and the implementation and management of process-driven ITSM systems. Prafull has acquired a unique blend of expertise in integrated areas of tools, process, governance, operations, and technology. He is the author of several methodologies and frameworks for IT service management that include multivendor ITIL frameworks, ITSM for Cloud computing, and Service Integration. Prafull's competencies and specializations include the area of merging engineering with service management, as this book manifests, and outsourcing business management.

Kavindra Sharma

Kavindra has spent over 30 years in the IT industry and 8 years in academics as faculty. He is graduate in Electronics & Communications engineering from Indore University and post-graduate in Computer Science from I.I.T. Bombay, India. He was a coder and designer in his early career and had developed many packages, systems, utilities and system software extensively in Unix and C environment during early 1980's. Later he managed large projects mainly on Mainframes involving development, maintenance and Y2K work. He was founder and leader of technology, innovation and consultancy units in various IT companies that he worked for. He taught computer science courses at Indore university as faculty during a five-year sabbatical. Retired from full-time employment, he is now an IT consultant and mentor to start-ups programs and a visiting faculty teaching IT, Strategy and Management related subjects.

References

(1974) Zen and the Art of Motorcycle Maintenance – An inquiry into Values (ZAMM), Robert M. Pirsig   ISBN 0-688-00230-7

(1975) The Mythical Man-Month, Brooks, Frederick P. Jr. ISBN 0-201-00650-2.

(1985) The secrets of Consulting – A Guide to Giving and Getting Advice Successfully, Gerald M Weinberg   ASIN: B004J35LHQ.

(1950) I, Robot
Isaac Asimov ISBN:978-0230-034433

(1980) Cosmos
Carl Sagan ISBN: 0-345-33135-4

(2013) Process excellence for IT Operations, Prafull Verma and Kalyan Kumar   ISBN-13: 978-0615877525

(2019) What it takes – Lessons in the Pursuit of Excellence, Stephen A. Swarzman   ISBN 978-1-4711-9349-1.

(2005) Paradox of Choice – Why More is Less, Barry Schwartz ISBN : 0-06-000568-8.

(2015) Software Asset Management: Understanding and Implementing an Optimal Solution, Prafull Verma and Kalyan Kumar
ISBN-13: 978-0692324264

(2018) Adapting to Digital Transformation: Design Sensible SLAs for Modern IT, Prafull Verma, Kalyan Kumar and Mohan Kewalramani
ISBN-13: 978-0692889169

(2005) The Wisdom of Crowds: Why the Many Are Smarter Than the Few, James Surowiecki   ISBN 978-0-349-11605-1

(2004) Does IT Matter? Information Technology and Corrosion of Competitive Advantage, Nicholas G Carr   ISBN: 978-1-5914-9444-0

(2015) The Hidden Life of Trees - What they feel and How they Communicate, Peter Wohlleben   ISBN: 9780670089345

www.ingramcontent.com/pod-product-compliance
Lightning Source LLC
Chambersburg PA
CBHW071359210526
45465CB00001B/169